WHAT PEOPLE REFERR.

"My real estate story was featured in the first book *"Becoming a Local Leader"*. My co-authors had amazing stories about their real estate journeys which were both inspiring and gave insight into the power of reciprocity. This book is as inspiring as the first one with new stories and ideas and is very well written. Whether you're at the beginning of your career or a seasoned vet you can take away something valuable that will bring you to the next level. I would highly recommend reading both! I wish that both of these books had existed when I started in the real estate business."

~ Pat Love, eXp Realty, Vancouver, British Columbia, Canada

"Referrals are the life blood of the real estate world. Without referrals, one's business is nothing more than a constant chase. Chasing after leads, chasing after ads or chasing after doors, it's all the same. These authors/agents have proven that their systems work as they fill their databases with quality buyers and sellers. Read this book and learn from the best"."

~Rich Gaasenbeek, CRO/IXACT Contact by Elm Street, Toronto, Ontario, Canada

“This book, Referral Secrets, ticks multiple boxes for growing your business through relationship building: mindset, variety, becoming a local leader, and appealing to those who care about their neighborhood. Businesspeople either have have a relationship mindset or a transactional mindset. Learning to be relational will make a huge difference in your business, especially when downturns in the economy happen. Not if, when. People will still buy and sell during downturns, they are much more likely to use a Realtor they already know, like and trust. This book, like its predecessor, Becoming a Local Leader: How to Grow Your Business by Giving Value to Your Community First, is a veritable cookbook and how to grow your business by referral. If one story doesn’t resonate with you, there is a variety of others which will. It will show you not just what to do, but HOW to do it. Lastly, many sellers have been in their neighborhood for many years, some decades. They care about their community and want to seek help from an agent who also cares about the neighborhood and knows it well. Referral Secrets will help you find clients with whom you have a connection. Starting a transaction with a warm and friendly referral will mean all the difference, not only to your bottom line, but also to the sales Experience.”

~ Chip Barkel, eXp Realty, Toronto, Ontario, Canada

"Becoming a Local Leader® is a meaningful way of becoming part of the fabric of the community you serve and do business in. Belonging in it and leading the way. Being a leader doesn’t just happen overnight as these authors/agents are tribute to. Study their words and apply them to your business. You'll become the leader you were meant to be."

~ Jane Castillo, Keller Williams, Los Angeles, California, USA

"I am a huge believer in providing targeted, purposeful value to my audience, clients, team members and coworkers and expecting nothing in return. Value is almost always reciprocated in some way, shape or form. This book captures the essence of many agents with the same mindset and philosophy as I do and they do a great job of explaining that in this book!! This is a great read for anyone struggling in their real estate career or thinking about getting started in any type of business. The information shared can be used in many different industries."

~ Monte Reyment, Symes Realty, Greenbay, Wisconsin, USA

"Do you have a job or do you have a business? Real estate agents often find themselves becoming order takers(job) vs community leaders(business). This book sets you on the right path for success as a business owner. There are so many examples of taking your business to the next level from discussing the difference between a Transactional model and a Relationship based approach. Give so you can Receive. Learn from these successful agents and how they do it right!"

~ Regan Sample, St Vrain Realty, Longmont, Colorado, USA

LOCAL LEADER®
REFERRAL SECRETS

HOW TO GROW YOUR REAL ESTATE BUSINESS
THROUGH RELATIONSHIPS & REFERRALS

GRANT FINDLAY-SHIRRAS

FOREWORD BY
YORK BAUR

Local Leader® - Referral Secrets

Published by: Grant Findlay-Shirras of Parkbench Inc.

Suite 320 - 171 East Liberty St.

Toronto, Ontario, Canada

M6K 3P6

www.parkbench.com

1st Edition: October 23rd, 2022

Design by: Christina Curkovic

Edited by: Grant Findlay-Shirras

ISBN 978-1-7778666-2-4

CONTENTS

FOREWORD

BY YORK BAUR

"Houses don't buy houses, people buy houses."

York Baur
CEO, MoxiWorks

As the CEO of MoxiWorks since 2012, I have been a part of an amazing journey with this company and have realized exponential growth with expansion to over 800 brokerage clients and growing, serving over 400,000 agents that makeup approximately 40% of all residential real estate transactions in the United States.

Moxiworks has existed as a standalone business for more than ten years. However, it originally grew out of a multi-generational brokerage called Windermere Real Estate. The fundamental premise of Windermere has always been *"High quality service and formation and curation of relationships."*

Why are relationships important? It is because 82% of a mature agent's business comes from their sphere of influence. We at Moxi-Works have 25+ years of technology experience that was built on the foundation to make the agent great with people who *know, like and trust them.* Especially in today's world of economic turbulence, our mission to help each agent become and stay relevant with their sphere is more important than ever.

History has proven that the housing market is cyclical and inevitably when the market is 'hot' it often attracts the hobbyists, the disrupters and all those people who are going to totally change and revolutionize the market. The fact is this 'revolution' simply never happens.

The reason this never happens, in my opinion, has two causes:

1. They are no two homes alike. Even a 'cookie cutter' home is different because of varying lots, views and neighbors.

2. It is the most financially and emotionally significant transaction most people will face in their lifetime.

Having said all this, you are not going to entrust this to some 'shmo' off the street. It would be like walking into a 'heart store' and ordering your open-heart surgery because it's on sale!

The data can speak for itself.

- Agent-assisted transactions remain at an all-time high-90% currently.

- The complexity of the transactions has also increased.

So why is the sphere of influence the key?

1. 90% of consumers post a *"I love my agent"* review after they have completed the transaction.

2. 12 months later, only 2 out of 10 can remember the agent's name.

This is because the majority of agents regard their clients as 'transactions' and move onto the next paycheck. So in essence, the mindset difference of the agent needs to change which will make *all the difference* in the world. This mindset shift can lead to better performance and more enjoyment in what you do. If you are not a 'people person' you have to question whether or not real estate is really your thing. Remember, people are your clients, not houses.

"Houses don't buy houses, people buy houses."

3. When it comes time to choose an agent, the average person will interview 1.2 agents before choosing. In essence, people pick the first agent they talk to.

As a real estate agent all you have to do is work with people, communicate with them regularly, stay relevant to them, and stay visible then they will pick you!

Let's have some fun with math. The average agent with MoxiWorks has 400 people in their database and of those approximately 10% or 40 will try to transact in a year. If you simply 'stay in front of them' and half of them choose you, well that's 20 sales!

Keep in mind, you have to constantly 'backfill' your sphere of influence as people move away, change lifestyles or their needs change. Growing your database is important and the Parkbench platform is a great example of how to grow your sphere at a more organic level. It also offers a way for people who do know you to refer you to people you don't know-yet.

When we witness a downturn market, such as the one in 2008-2009 and the one we are in now(2022), we will expect a culling of the herd, so to speak. This type of 'reckoning' is a good thing as it has and will cause the non-sphere oriented agents and hobbyists to go elsewhere and leave behind the agents who do good for their clients and communities.

Being a relational agent offers you so much more than a sustainable business, it offers you a lifestyle that most people would dream of. Imagine getting a text at 11:00 at night from a stranger asking about the tile in the bathroom on a listing you have never seen OR having a coffee with a client and laughing about the crazy tile in the bathroom that you know needs to go. Which one would you choose?

At MoxiWorks we honor the relationship value in one of two ways. Firstly, we do not pretend a computer can be a substitute for a person. Secondly, what we are doing is keeping track of stuff and reminding humans to do things that only a human can do! For instance, our CRM is for customer relationship management, with the emphasis on the relationship. A computer is great at collecting data and calculating marketplace trends, but it can't pour you a cup of coffee when you meet for the first time or present a report and answer questions.

The reason why Grant Findlay-Shirras, CEO of Parkbench, and I are in a business partnership is because Parkbench fulfills an important additive role to what we do at MoxiWorks. In terms of fostering these relationships, the visibility of these relationships and the digital marketing behind all of this, the automation takes the load off the agents so they can spend their time doing the relationship piece that only the agent can do. Technology at its highest and best use is for productivity's sake, not for technology alone.

Real estate is a relationship business and the stories contained within these pages are highly compatible with this notion. I encourage you to read these stories, invest yourself in the intellectual content and synthesize the pieces that are relevant and which you can successfully put into practice.

Best of luck!

York Baur

REACH OUT TO YORK BAUR

moxiworks.com
york@moxiworks.com
@moxiworks

MORE ABOUT YORK

York is a first-generation American and son of German and Swiss immigrants. York was accustomed to a lifestyle guided by structure, systems and process, as his father was a doctor who upheld strict values within the household.

As a pilot, York was accustomed to the checklists and systems that are a daily regimen of this profession. He soon took these practices into the corporate world where he became successful in implementing these into businesses in need of expansion. His reputation led him to MoxiWorks where he has enjoyed 10 years as their CEO. In his words: *"MoxiWorks was the overnight success that took ten years."*

CHAPTER 1

REALTOR®

"Whether you are buying a home or selling one, it is imperative that you choose the right real estate agent for your needs and desires."

Jim Crawford
Pottstown, PA

GET TO KNOW JIM CRAWFORD

I am a Realtor ® with Better Homes and Gardens Real Estate Community Realty in Pottstown, PA. My business focus is on Eastern Pennsylvania. As a U.S Navy Veteran, I changed careers not long ago and now I have been actively working in this industry for three plus years and am honored to be the recipient of the P.A.I.G.E. Award (Passion, Authenticity, Inclusion, Growth and Excellence). I hold the following certifications that allow me to service my clients better:

Expect Better® certified, Commitment to Excellence (C2EX) certified, At Home with Diversity® (AHWD) certified, ePRO® digital marketing certified, Pricing Strategy Advisor (PSA) certified, Short Sales and Foreclosure Resource® (SFR®) certified, VA Loan certified — thevaloan.org.

In my spare time, I coach soccer with the Pottsgrove Soccer Club and Pottsgrove High School. I also hold memberships with the Elks, VFW, and American Legion.

I live with my wife, Lauren and I am a proud father of James (son) and Bailey (daughter). We are kept busy with our family pet, Franklin the Boston Terrier.

REALTOR®

JIM CRAWFORD

Whether you are buying a home or selling one, it is imperative that you choose the right real estate agent for your needs and desires. It's no secret that the real estate industry has a wide range of services and offerings for people, but the most important investment of your life deserves a dedicated professional to help you 'unpack' everything you need to accomplish your goals.

There are generally two types of real estate professionals in terms of how they approach their business and client's needs.

1. Transactional: This type of agent typically focuses on the numbers. In many cases, their goal is to get you to and over the finish line quickly and with as little interaction or effort as possible.

- Uses generic email templates to follow up.
- Rarely phones you, instead relies on team members or subordinates to communicate with you.
- Boasts about past statistics instead of understanding your unique needs.
- Drives the splashy expensive car to show off their 'success.'

- Takes too long to respond to your questions or concerns if they respond at all
- Shows up late because they are "too busy."

2. Relationship: These people are fun to work with and truly have your needs in the forefront. They prefer to forge a relationship with you from the start and will bend over backwards to get you everything you need. What to look for:

- They will return phone calls or texts promptly.
- They are great communicators and guide you through each step.
- Will get to know you and your family.
- Will anticipate your needs.
- Have a large network of industry professionals to help you during and after the sale.
- Is often found volunteering in your community.
- Has a smile on their face!

Things to look for:

- Great communication - in order to truly be successful in this market, it is imperative that the client and agent are fully on the same page.
- Reliable - an agent must be on time for appointments and must do what they say.
- Rapport - if the interaction doesn't feel right, then it isn't. Find an agent that makes you feel good. Don't settle because of past statistics.
- Reviews - check out an agent's google reviews, you can tell alot based on what a past client was willing to publish for the world to see.

NAVIGATING THE TREACHEROUS WATERS

As most of us have been aware, the real estate market has been on quite a different path these last few years. It's been crazy to say the least. People are needing more direction and help than ever before because the market is so volatile. They need an advocate vs a paper pusher.

Buyers and sellers need a skilled negotiator that champions their individual transaction as if it was their own in order to succeed in an unbalanced market. I have certainly been more intentional with my efforts in order to help clients navigate these treacherous waters. I have put more time into creating sustainable relationships with clients, other agents and industry folks in order to stand out from the crowd.

AVOID LISTING PITFALLS

Although listing your house may seem straightforward, it does warrant some discussion, in particular with respect to pitfalls you may encounter. Top of mind, every transaction is a business transaction not an emotional one. I understand that your home has possibly years of memories with laughter and tears shed and you have strong ties to it. My job is to help set aside those memories, for a moment, and deal with the task at hand.

Dotting i's and crossing t's and attention to detail is crucial because we are dealing with sensitive legal documents and processes. Thankfully, my military background has served me well with organization and timeliness!

At the end of the day, price does matter-on both sides of the contract. Pricing too high can leave your house sitting idly while others around you are being scooped up. Pricing too low might be leaving money on the table. I often chuckle when I hear things like, *"My neighbor sold hers for $$$."* Or, *"I heard from Billy's father's sister that we should sell it for $$$."* The right agent can help you price your home based on local knowledge and experience to ensure that you sell quickly and profitably.

Another thing to be aware of is getting information off the internet.

For example, Zillow offers an online service that determines the value of your home through their software programs. These can be very misleading because it does not take into account the whole picture. Pricing is a combination of art and science that only a human being can offer.

Last but certainly not least, selling a home is in most cases the single largest financial transaction in a person's life. This transaction should not be left in the hands of a discount broker. Im always reminded of the below quote whenever I hear that a client is considering this option:

We offer 3 kinds of service: GOOD-CHEAP-FAST- But you can only pick two…

- GOOD & CHEAP won't be FAST
- FAST & GOOD won't be CHEAP
- CHEAP & FAST won't be GOOD.

BUYER BEWARE

As a buyer in the market, there are a few things you should keep in mind when shopping for a new home. Keep in mind, there may be some variation from state to state, but for the most part they should remain the same.

The lender matters. Local lenders add value to transactions in many ways but one to note is that they too are from the area and are invested in the success of the community.

Setting a budget or price expectation in the beginning is critical so that you and your agent can shop strategically. Getting a mortgage pre-approval, prior to looking at homes is crucial in the current market.

Shopping around for a mortgage can be daunting, but there are a few pieces of the puzzle worth mentioning. Look for a lender that has a good reputation vs a good interest rate. You want to ensure that the processing will close on time and done efficiently. Ask your agent for a list of 2-3 recommendations.

Once you receive your preapproval, its not over yet. You still have to have money for closing costs and down payment.

I often refer to the book, "Start With Why" by Simon Sinek. It is important to understand the needs of clients to be able to help most effectively. If I am able to uncover the why behind a need or want, I can help uncover additional options.

I also use tours of houses to create a feedback loop and a way to drill down to the fundamentals of what is required to create a successful ending.

IN CLOSING

I am so fortunate to have so many people to thank for supporting and encouraging me along my journey. My family and friends are on the top of my list. My wife, Lauren is a wonderful person who is by my side every step of the way. My two children, James and Bailey keep me feeling young!

Lastly, I want to thank my wonderful clients over the years. You are a big reason why I get up in the mornings with a smile on my face!

Jim Crawford

REACH OUT TO JIM CRAWFORD

Jim Crawford - Realtor, ePRO, AHWD, PSA, C2EX, SFR
Better Homes and Gardens Real Estate Community Realty
Cell/Text (267)768-7676
jimcrawfordrealestate@gmail.com
www.jimcrawfordrealestate.com
https://www.facebook.com/jimcrawfordrealestate

WHAT CLIENTS ARE SAYING ABOUT JIM

"In terms of business, Jim is well researched, well connected, and goes above and beyond to ensure the satisfaction of both you as a buyer and/or seller. Professionally speaking, he is undoubtedly one of the best. But what makes Jim absolutely shine is who he is as a person. He is thoughtful, patient, and is truly representative of someone who cares about our community. There is no doubt in my mind that you'd be in the right hands when working with Jim. Highly recommended!"

~Betsy T

"Jim was truly incredible. Recommended to me by family and friends, Jim was a fantastic realtor and helped us immensely. My fiancé and I were first time home buyers and Jim took us through the entire process and never left us with unanswered questions. Being quick to respond and making himself available at all hours of the day and weekends, we found our dream home. Jim was willing to work with our busy schedules and made sure we felt like his only client

while juggling others without us realizing. Although my fiancé and I were stressed, Jim kept us calm and always had his eyes open for our dream home. When we didn't think it would happen, his optimism prevailed and the home was found. If I ever need a realtor again or have friends who need one, I'm sending them to Jim!"

~Maxwell B.

"Being a first time home buyer, was a little intimidating at first. But with the help of Jim and staff, he made the process much easier than I could even imagine. Jim was professional, organized , informative, flexible and most importantly friendly. With the help of Jim I can now say I am finally now a part of the first time home buyer club! Jim we did it!"

~Gina P.

CHAPTER 2

WHY NOT US?

"Our personal mantra is "Success is a byproduct of relationships." Relationships of all sorts, including business owners, business alliances, and most importantly, our clients help shape our success."

Joe & Jocelyn Maggi
Belchertown, MA

GET TO KNOW JOE & JOCELYN MAGGI

We are a husband and wife team that was created in 2017. We're now the managing partners of the Maggi Realty Group of Century 21 North East! Joe has been an agent for over 30 years in Western MA. Jocelyn was an agent in the Kansas City area and joined Century 21 when she moved to Western MA. We assist both buyers and sellers in real estate transactions. Joe has a great experience in home renovations and construction, and together we have considerable knowledge of new construction. We work together to provide the highest quality service to our clients!

WHY NOT US?

JOE & JOCELYN MAGGI

SUCCESS IS A BYPRODUCT

Our personal mantra is *"Success is a byproduct of relationships."* Relationships of all sorts, including business owners, business alliances, and most importantly, our clients help shape our success. Each of us has been successful on our own merits, however, since 2017 when we joined forces, we have been unstoppable. As small business owners, we have a deep appreciation for what it takes to create and build one's dreams from the grassroots. I [Jocelyn] previously owned a fitness center and Joe owned and still does, a paint/construction business. Hard work and determination are no strangers to us, and our real estate business is no exception.

I've [Joe] been a real estate agent for 30+ years and I call Belchertown my home. Jocelyn and I met here in Belchertown, and we soon realized we wanted to merge our efforts and create a team of our own. Jocelyn previously had her real estate license in Kansas City, so she got a new license in Massachusetts.

As the local Century 21 office in Western MA was bought out by another company, our current mission is working on resurrecting the Century 21 brand and making it stronger than ever. We believe in the

Century 21 company because it has so much to offer in terms of support and guidance.

OUR MARRIAGE MAKES OUR BUSINESS STRONGER

Joe has been fundamental in terms of helping me believe in myself and increasing my confidence too. His self-assurance and support are vital to me and our business. I know I can always lean on him for anything, and he will be there for me. *"He is my rock and my best friend!"*

I love working with Jocelyn because I get to spend more time with the love of my life. I have never had a partner who I respect as much. She is as dedicated to our work as she is to our marriage. I get to work with someone who shares my passion for real estate and shares every part of my life with me. When we are done with work I can take my best friend, partner, and love out for a date and enjoy her company more!

OUR TURNING POINT

As most businesspeople are aware, the start-up phase always takes a lot of effort and determination. As we began working together, the real estate business was not paying our bills, so Jocelyn and I continued to climb ladders and paint houses to make up for the shortfall. It wasn't until we had our aha moment that we realized we could rock our business like other top producers in our company. We were watching other people rise to the top and we turned to each other and said, *"Why not us?"* This is our motto, and it is ingrained in our souls!

Our talents and skills complement each other to a 'T'. We don't have assigned roles, but we do manage our strong suits. For instance, Jocelyn is a superstar with market analysis and the administrative side of the business, and I have an eye for construction and work the showings. Today, many of our tasks are blended and our business success stems from our passion about working with and helping clients through their journeys.

TODAY'S TEAM

A bit of a back story about how we built our own team. In 2017, we were on a team at Century 21. That company was bought out and later we were approached by Century 21 North East to lead our own team. Again, we were guided by our mantra *"Why not us?"* So, we jumped at the opportunity and haven't looked back since.

Our team, Maggi Realty Group, consists of eight people, including Joe's daughter, Alyssa and we are expecting three more to jump on board. We are experiencing some growing pains, but we are managing by adding a marketing director to our roster. This is allowing us to step back from the daily marketing activities and move into more of a mentorship role for our young and newly-formed team members.

We foster and encourage a culture of cohesiveness and openness within our group. I [Jocelyn] know what a new agent has to go through, so I embrace this time by showing them the ropes and imparting my knowledge to them. I know I can help them get across the finish line.

I [Joe] feel like our team is family. We do group outings and share family cookouts together. We have a real 'play hard, work hard' ethic in the office which everyone appreciates.

REAL ESTATE IS IN OUR BLOOD

Growing up my [Jocelyn] Aunt and Uncle were involved in real estate, and I always looked up to them. In college, I took a few real estate classes because they intrigued me. When I got married, my first husband and I moved around a lot with the military, so I was in a supportive role with our children at home. When I met Joe, I decided to get my license as I wanted something for myself.

I [Joe] have always used real estate as a byproduct of my other businesses. For example, I used my license to flip my own houses and to sell my renovation clients' houses as well.

For both of us, we are building a legacy that will provide us with residual income well into our 'Golden years.'

BEHIND THE SCENES

To us, a local leader is someone who gives back to the community without a personal gain attached to it. A person who is genuine, selfless, and out there making things happen is a leader in my mind [Jocelyn]. I'm [Joe] more of a 'behind the scenes' kinda guy as I am in the background subtly creating change for my world.

I [Jocelyn] think Joe is a 'Mayor' of Belchertown because we can't go out anywhere without being stopped by a passerby who recognizes him. I [Joe] like making connections with people so when I'm out for a walk I always say 'hi' to those within earshot! Recently, we were out for a walk and Joe said hi to a couple who stopped to chat. It turns out they were moving here and needed a real estate agent — guess who had their card ready?

OPPORTUNITY KNOCKED

When Century 21 North East approached us to create a new team and give presence back to Western Massachusetts, we were ecstatic. We knew it was going to be a lot of hard work, but we accepted the challenge. We do give recognition to our past broker, Century 21 Hometown Associates, because if it wasn't for them, we wouldn't be where we are today. However, it was our turn to become leaders, so we embraced it.

The Covid pandemic was all but kind to many businesses. We currently own a commercial property and during the pandemic, we lost some leases due in part to businesses not being able to sustain themselves. Century 21 North East offered to lease a big space from us in this building which helped us immensely as well. They really came through for us on so many levels. They gave us extensive training, support, and tools to help us create a team that we are so proud of. They upheld all their promises, and we did too. It was a real win-win opportunity for us, and we are so grateful.

LEADING WITH CONFIDENCE

Some key factors have contributed to our success that are worth mentioning. Both of us are easy to approach, accessible, and can connect with clients quickly. People appreciate that we are true to our word and regard our relationships with utmost importance.

We are highly responsive to any and all questions that come our way, even if they are not directly related to our business. Consistency and self-confidence are attributes that we hold steadfast in our daily workings. In addition, people appreciate that we are low-key and pressure-free and that we will not oversell them.

We approach our first meetings like we would a first date; there is no need to put a ring on it before we have a coffee first! So, we don't have agent contracts signed right away because we want the relationship to develop first. We are often faced with talking 'people off the ledge' because most people have anxiety around home buying and selling. In particular, many of our clients are first-time home buyers who tend to be 'nervous nellies' and excited about their new venture. We offer a great deal of support and guidance because we know we will be spending a lot of time with them and want to ensure they have a great experience.

FOLLOW THROUGH

In just about any sales role the kiss of death is giving up too soon. The stats are dismal when it comes to looking at the behaviors of salespeople and the real estate industry is no exception. This, we believe, is due in large part to the fact that people fear rejection, and no one wants to get hung up on or yelled at over the phone. With the advent of technology, many people are hiding behind their social media posts and emails. You can't grow a business this way.

I [Joe] believe you have to get out of your comfort zone to progress at any level. Do things that make you feel uncomfortable and you will soon realize it isn't so bad after all. Follow up and follow through with every conversation, every email, and every inquiry you get.

ADVICE TO OUR YOUNGER SELVES

If I [Jocelyn] were to start over I would believe in myself more and have more confidence that I can succeed. I know now that I can take a lot so I would say, "Take more, you've got this!" It was a long journey and a lot of pieces had to be put together for me to get here, but I don't have a single regret.

As a young person, I [Joe] thought I'd be dead by age 21 but here I am alive and kicking! I didn't have the aptitude then like I do now, so I couldn't see very far down the road. I did, however, have strong family values and a good work ethic which were instilled in me by my Italian parents. *"If I work 12 hours, then I only worked half a day"* — I still hear that ringing in my ears.

Having such a young team allows us to give them advice because we lived and worked through it all ourselves. Again, follow-through is fundamental to success in our world. *"I called and left a message, and nobody called me back,"* doesn't fly with us.

Training is another very important aspect that we teach our team to embrace. Our company, Century 21 North East, takes training to a whole new level. There is almost too much to absorb, so pacing oneself is key. When an agent starts with us, we encourage them to join the weekly new and experienced agent training where they can talk about their struggles and share strengths and wins!

My [Joe] daughter, Alyssa is on our team, and she struggles with putting it out there. We don't want her to be a 'best-kept secret', so we encourage her to take steps to help her gain confidence. Wherever you are, you have to talk to people and let them know you are an agent.

START PROSPECTING

We started working with Parkbench to help bridge the gap in our business. We recognize that video is where it's at in today's marketing and the use of Parkbench's platform will help push our marketing to a new level. This will also help us get to know more people and expand our sphere of influence. We are also looking forward to increasing our brand recognition and putting Century 21 North East back on the map!

The interview process will get us out in front of people which we can leverage to increase our prospecting. This is a really fun way to do business and we get to do it together!

We would like to thank Jim D'Amico, our broker, and the D'Amico family from Century 21 North East for investing in us and giving us the opportunity to grow our team!

Joe & Jocelyn Maggi

REACH OUT TO JOE & JOCELYN MAGGI

Joe Maggi: (413) 530-4657
Jocelyn Maggi: (413) 461-5042
Shared Email: joeandjocelynsoldours@gmail.com

WHAT CLIENTS ARE SAYING ABOUT JOE & JOCELYN

"Jocelyn and Joe made the selling experience so smooth. When selling was just an idea, they came out to advise us on what needed to be fixed. Then when we were finally ready to list, they were with us every step of the way, from providing an up-to-date market analysis, answering so many questions, presenting us with multiple offers, and walking us through the closing process. We can't say enough good things about Jocelyn and Joe and highly recommend their team for any buyer or seller."

~Angela T.

"Joe Maggi was the best! He was thorough and professional and great to work with. He kept us apprised about available appointments and always let us know as soon as a new one came on the market. He was honest and forthright, and really cared about us. If he wasn't available, Jocelyn would step in. We always had someone there to take care of us. Great communication throughout the process. Will definitely work with them again and very highly recommend!"

~Anonymous

"Selling our home with Joe was a pleasure. He is extremely knowledgeable and was helpful throughout the entire process. Our questions were met with answers at lightning speed. I would not hesitate to work with Joe again."

~Christopher G.

"Jocelyn and Joe were great to work with, they were responsive, honest, knowledgeable and reliable. They were also patient with us as first time home buyers and helped us through the process of buying our first home which is a great house in our desired area. I would highly recommend them."

~E.W.B

"Joe and Jocelyn were professional, knowledgeable and helped make my first time buying a home a smooth process. I strongly recommend them to anyone looking to sell or purchase a home!"

~Laura L.

CHAPTER 3

LEAD WITH A COMPLIMENT

"We are not trading time for money, we are trading the value of, support, knowledge and confidence, which comes from making informed decisions about real estate."

Matt Mundell
Kingston, ON

GET TO KNOW MATT MUNDELL

Together with his wife Gillianne, Matt is raising 3 beautiful daughters in a home filled with love, a mindset of inclusion, and an attitude of reciprocity, accompanied by a steady reminder that we all can grow from applying the golden rule to our lives daily. The golden rule is "treat others how you would like to be treated".

The Mundell family is a generational family who has lived in the Kingston area for years. Matt and his sister Jessica's parents, Mike and Linda Mundell, all started a small retail business in Kingston where their family worked together. Matt and Jessica learned the value of caring for people, hard work, and giving back to the community by supporting people and others in business on the path of life we all share.

These lessons have helped to guide Matt into becoming a successful Real Estate agent in Kingston and surrounding areas, which he is humbled and grateful to have grown with the support of many families, friends, and clients. 'With the knowledge of working together, a community is stronger, and with the support of one another, people can truly accomplish anything. This is a guiding principle in Matt's life, both professionally and personally. These values have proven invaluable to him in his life.

Should you find yourself in Kingston please do reach out. Matt has a wealth of local knowledge about Kingston and the surrounding areas, and would be happy to speak with you, welcome you to Kingston, and help in any way he can.

LEAD WITH A COMPLIMENT

MATT MUNDELL

Known as "the Limestone city" Kingston has a rich history of culture and nostalgia . . . evidenced by our cobblestone downtown streets and historic 19th-century limestone architecture. Located centrally between our nation's capital, Ottawa and Toronto, Kingston is the base for exploring the Thousand Islands and St. Lawrence River. Preserving our heritage is always top of mind yet Kingston remains acutely aware of the importance of keeping with the times and staying up to date with the conveniences of modern technology and amenities, after all, Elon Musk studied at Queen's University here. For those who may not know, he is the founder of companies such as Tesla and SpaceX. While I am at it, I should also mention that Kingston is home to one of Canada's most well-known bands, The Tragically Hip, which has influenced millions with their music.

More recently, Kingston has brought a new rock band onto the scene called "The Glorious Sons", which is proof that rock and roll will never die. They are well worth a YouTube search. With all this world class talent, Kingston remains a humble town, proud of its heritage and true to its roots. Another attraction includes our fresh food outdoor market in the rear yard of our City Hall, affectionately called "Springer Market Square", where vendors come during the summer months to showcase their fine local foods, crafts, and jewelry. During the winter months, the market square turns into an outdoor hockey/skating rink, complete with its own Zamboni!

Kingston values community and this town makes a conscious effort to bring people together with events like "Movies in the Square", where people gather to watch a flick outside in the market square during warm summer evenings. Blues Fest is another widely popular event during the summer months. Of course, I must mention that there is always lots of excitement from our local hockey team, the Kingston Frontenac. With so much going on, it is no wonder Kingston is a hub for tourists and newly-transitioning homeowners seeking a more relaxed lifestyle for themselves and their families.

CANADA'S FOODIE CAPITAL

Fun fact: Kingston has the greatest number of restaurants in Canada and is only second to New Orleans in all North America! For the true foodie at heart, we have everything on the menu — literally.

It's never a long drive to any of our favourite restaurants, including our number one choice, Gina Sushi followed closely by Lavallee's Cookery, where we love a home-cooked meal (outside of our own kitchen, that is). When we are in the mood for pizza, Paradiso always delivers on quality and service! If it is a summer patio you are seeking, there are many to choose from. Some of the local favourites are Red House, Dianne's Fish Shack and Smokehouse for all things seafood, and if it's a woodfired pizza you crave, Woodenheads never disappoints. With so many great restaurants here, it is hard to name just a few.

WHY KINGSTON?

Having grown up in this quaint town, I have never had the urge to live anywhere else. I love the small-town feel and enjoy walking down the street waving to my neighbours and catching up on the latest town news.

We take great pride in preserving the historical features and architecture of our buildings and national treasures. Our community is filled with kind, supportive, and involved people who would help anyone at a moment's notice. We work together to build our community and welcome anyone wanting to call it home.

Family, food, and fun are the heart of our community. I love to fish in nearby lakes and rivers, which are bountiful in this neck of the woods.

ALL ROADS LEAD HOME

Being part of the family business growing up meant a lot to me and it helped pave the way for my real estate business. Our family owned and operated a food service company that put people and the community above the bottom line. My parents and their parents always believed that everyone should be fed, clothed, and housed. "No one should be without."

Later on, I decided to leave the 'business nest' and joined a home developer and worked on a framing crew. We were a small crew of four and we set about creating a livelihood for our own growing families. As time went on, I began to realize that with being in the construction business, I was far removed from the active interactions with people. I wasn't fulfilled.

Although I appreciated the value of having these people in my life, I was missing something. That 'something' was social interaction. Don't get me wrong, I appreciated what we had but it wasn't fulfilling my need to interact with people. I like to meet new people and create bonds with them, but this business didn't quite meet that desire for me.

After I reassessed my desires, I headed straight into real estate in 2009 and haven't looked in the rearview mirror since. By the way, my back isn't sore anymore and I'm loving that!

MY AHA MOMENT

Moving from building homes to selling them was a natural progression for me. However, it wasn't until a few years in that I had my 'aha' moment.

> *"We are not trading time for money, we are trading the value of, support, knowledge and confidence, which comes from making informed decisions about real estate."*

Trading value, support, and knowledge with my clients is what they need to help create a success story for them. Buying a home is a highly charged, emotional endeavor and it's my duty to understand that and support my clients in every way possible. It's my job to make the process enjoyable, rewarding, and fulfilling, by guiding clients with the help of other trusted professionals. We take the right steps and make the home search and purchase as stress-free as possible.

GENERATIONAL REAL ESTATE

Working in the real estate industry in Frontenac County, Kingston is a unique experience mainly because it is both generational and transitioning simultaneously. Families tend to stay close to each other and remain loyal to their local community. At the same time, we are seeing more and more young people moving into the area. They are mainly coming from Toronto and Ottawa — the larger city center, in favour of a quieter and more remote lifestyle.

Kingston is a tourist town located on the Eastern shores of Lake Ontario. Many businesses thrive in this environment, especially restaurants and historical sites like the Old Fort Henry and the museums. Also, the proximity to the Thousand Islands is a huge draw for tourists and locals alike. This area is also the gateway to the Rideau Canal waterway, which is recognized by UNESCO as a world heritage site and offers literally thousands of kilometers of shoreline to explore.

The cottage country, South Frontenac in particular, is home to so many crystal-clear lakes and rivers and is definitely a huge part of the real estate industry in these parts. The city dwellers love to get away from the hustle and enjoy their time with family and friends in a relaxed and fun environment.

SUCCESS LEAVES CLUES

Pay close attention to people around you who are successful in their field, as they will leave a string of clues for you to learn from. For instance, Mary Campeau, a life-long real estate agent in Kingston, was a great mentor when I was starting fresh into my new career. Mary always makes time for her clients, she listens to them, and hears their concerns. She was never too busy to take time to hear what someone had to say. Her guidance and patience will always be appreciated. What I have learned most throughout my career is to be consistent and methodical. Inconsistency will kill a business almost instantly but if you create a system and have a genuine concern for the well-being of your clients every day, you can't help but be successful.

Another colloquialism I live by is: *"The art is to conceal the art."* This is to say, people want to buy a home, but they don't want to know you are selling it to them. Sounds confusing? It is simple really. This can be done by speaking of the benefits a property offers to a particular client, tell them why it is a good fit, and what about it will increase their enjoyment of life and time spent there. Also, be truthful because if it is not a fit and you see downfalls, it is important to point these out. People are making important decisions and it is not always easy to think of everything. So, talk with them and listen to their reactions as this will help them realize whether the property is right for them, or if they should keep shopping. Create a mindset of never selling to people. I know what you are thinking . . . "But my job is to sell." How about this slant? My job is to provide, support, and nurture my clients. Craft your story and repeat it a hundred times before testing it out on others. It will become as natural as breathing — you don't have to think about it, it just happens.

THERE IS NO THEM, THERE IS JUST US

Life never turns out the way your 18-year-old self believes it will and I am no exception. At times I struggle with mental health issues and have learned that it's okay! Learning to cope with those days where I just don't feel like getting out of bed or my self-confidence takes a beating is all part of my journey. One soon finds out who is there for both the good times and the hard times. I thank my family and friends wholeheartedly for their love and support. Understanding that you are not alone in this struggle is one of the keys to overcoming it. The best advice one can give to someone who struggles with a mental health issue is to say, *"It is okay; you are not alone."*

DON'T SWEAT THE SMALL STUFF

I learned a very valuable lesson early in my career. Basically, it was to never sweat the small stuff. People often get hung up on the little things that really shouldn't matter. They can't see the forest for the trees because they are laser-focused on one item that is stopping them from progressing. I'll give you an example of a time one of my real estate deals fell apart and what I could have done to help prevent it. (If I only knew then what I know now!)

It was down to the wire as I was working on closing a deal with my buyer client. Both the seller and buyer got their backs up over the washer and dryer. They both felt they were being bullied and stood their ground and I recognized that egos were playing a large part in this. I should have handled it differently. I should have engaged myself more as a moderator and bridged the gap to offer each side their point of view without letting the whole thing go off the rails. The whole deal collapsed over a $4000 difference. The solution could have been handled better by me and the co-operating REALTOR®. If we had worked quicker to recognize that the issue was never about the washer and dryer but instead about pride standing in the way, we could have softened this situation and collaborated with one another to find a solution instead of letting the deal fall apart. When we all give a little, we all come out ahead.

CALL THEM BY NAME

It's such a simple thing to do but so few people actually do it. Calling someone by their first name creates an immediate bond with them and can help create trust and likability towards you.

As a leader in one's community, I believe there are four key attributes that help differentiate oneself from the competition. These are:

- Honesty
- Integrity
- Passion
- Understanding

People can see a false front from a mile away, so stay transparent with your clients and don't deviate from your personal brand.

JOIN A TEAM

Having been in the business for many years now, I can list the 'shoulda, coulda, and woulda.' Joining a team of professionals is one thing I regret not doing early on and here's why.

I 'shoulda' joined a team from the start. Instead, I sat behind the desk waiting for the phone to ring, and guess what? It didn't. My bills were piling up, but my calendar wasn't filling up. Teams can help you strategize leads and conversions and offer a support system that you can't get elsewhere.

I 'coulda' been part of a larger purpose or goals that often come with being on a team.

I 'woulda' done it if I had known the true value of investing in other people. Creating a small circle of like-minded people would have helped me immensely.

LEAD WITH A COMPLIMENT

A compliment sets the tone and tends to bring down social guards that we have either consciously or subconsciously put up so, it is huge, to

"Compliment off the bat!" This can be as simple as "I love your hairstyle" or "You have a really unique accent." An important thing to note is that for that compliment to 'land' properly don't dwell on it. Just say it, let the person respond, and then move on. It needs to be genuine and authentic. It needs to be considered an act of kindness.

WHAT WORKS FOR ME

When I first started in 2009, I contacted 'for sale by owners' with the intent to show them the value of my services. I knew I had to have the 'right' conversations with them as they are very leery of real estate agents. I often found that these sellers were, and still are, simply misinformed about the true services a Realtor® can bring to the table.

I would ask them to show me around their house so I could be better informed about what they were offering. If I did have a buyer in mind, then I would ask "when would be a good closing date for you?" Once I entered their house, I could start building a rapport with them but I kept it genuine and honest. I got listing clients as a result of these interactions.

Small items of value like magnetic business cards can be worthwhile. They tend to 'stick' around longer as people find a useful spot on their fridge for them. I also like to make specialized items for some of my clients who refer to my business. At Christmas, I make wreaths for their front doors. They appreciate the time I have put in. Smoked trout is one of my favourite gifts to give. As a fisherman, this is especially near and dear to my heart.

Social media has also been useful in growing my business. My Parkbench website offers a place to showcase interviews and videos in support of my fellow business owners in my community. As I meet new people and they get to know me, the value behind this website grows every day.

One of my favourite community events to help with is the local food drive. I get great joy out of serving and helping the less fortunate. Contribution is relevant and it is central to my core values.

ADVICE TO MY YOUNGER SELF

I've learned over the years not to be so hard on myself. Sometimes I can be my own worst enemy and need to shake myself to correct this negative thinking. Being self-aware and critical can be helpful if it creates a positive outcome. I have become better at letting go and not dwelling on things that don't really matter.

You may be sorry you spoke, sorry you stayed or left, or sorry you won or lost, perhaps. But as you go through life you will find you're never sorry you were kind.

DO'S AND DON'TS

Some simple rules that I live by:

Do:

- Get out there and meet new people. Every. Single. Day.
- Have 10 different conversations every day.
- Spend more time and money on training.
- Read and follow Brian Buffini.
- Get a coach. They can help steer you in the right direction and hold you accountable.
- Work with Parkbench. The Law of Reciprocity is key to the success of my efforts.

Don't:

- Control People — allow them to be part of the decision-making. This empowers them and builds confidence.
- Buy leads — EVER.
- Overspend on marketing, especially at the beginning of your career.

LAST THOUGHTS

Entering my 13th year in this business I consider myself a lucky man. Have I learned a ton? YES. Have I had fun? YES. Would I change anything from my past? NO.

If you are considering a career in real estate, I would encourage you to do it! It has been an amazing time in my life, and the rewards are many. It can be intimidating and often bewildering at first, but remember to be yourself, be real, and be prepared. People will work with you if you are genuine, honest, and prepared. Do not get offended when your friends and family don't flock to you for their real estate needs as this takes time, and it is only time and consistent effort that will grow your business.

Your strength and determination will flourish, as will a feeling of inner peace, given the knowledge that you did this yourself and it was not simply handed to you. Also, please keep in mind that success is not only measured by the number of deals you do or the money in your pocket, but also by the lives you touch and the way you treat people on this path of life we all share.

I am indebted to my family and close friends for their love and support in the good times but especially in the tough times. To name a few, my wife Gillianne, my parents Mike and Linda, and many great friends that I am so truly blessed to have in my life.

Matt Mundell

REACH OUT TO MATT MUNDELL

Website: www.Kingstonsold.com
Email: mmundell1@gmail.com
Direct 613-540-1037

WHAT CLIENTS ARE SAYING ABOUT MATT

"Matt Mundell is an outstanding REALTOR ® who possesses excellent communication skills that truly sets him apart from his peers. Matt was extremely helpful, knowledgeable, and responsive as our listing agent. He is so organized and quick to answer every question in the home buying and selling process. His professionalism, expertise, and excellent interpersonal skills work synergistically to make him a wonderful representative for anyone looking to buy or sell a home. The thing we appreciated most about Matt was his patience and ability to provide sound advice. I will recommend him to any of my friends and family members. If you're looking for someone to truly look out for your best interest as well as help you navigate through the Kingston housing market Matt is the agent for you."

~Kim P. & Stephen B.

"Matt made us feel like family. From giving us experienced advice on what to keep an eye out for, to having fun and helping us relax, and feel rest assured so we could enjoy this special life milestone. This is why we always suggest Matt Mundell, because he is the guy you want on your side. Thank you Matt for sharing your knowledge and passion with us, and helping us plant our roots!"

~Dave and Tania

CHAPTER 4

INSPIRED LIVING: YOUR HOME, OUR MISSION

"As with our family, our approach to our business is very much generational. We walk our clients through the whole process of not only home ownership but the journey beyond, one step at a time. The relationships we foster are what make us tick. Our desire to be there for our clients throughout their lifespans is really at the heart of our business."

Laura Jewett
Scottsdale, AZ

GET TO KNOW LAURA JEWETT

Laura Jewett is a Native Arizonan and has been a professional REALTOR® since January 2001 serving the greater Phoenix area. With a passion for all things real estate, she offers a true concierge approach to real estate for her clients, with expansive experience in design, rehab, fix and flip, construction, investment, rental, vacation rental and many other aspects of real estate.

Laura is a top producer in the industry and is dedicated to providing superior customer service to her clients. She has been honored and humbled by previous clients' testimonials of her service to them which she invites you to read at www.InspiredLivingCollective.com.

Accolades: Laura attended the University of Arizona and graduated Magna Cum Laude with Honors with double majors in Marketing and Entrepreneurship. She has always excelled academically and continues that thirst for knowledge in her real estate career having attained many credentials and specialized knowledge in areas including land sales, distressed properties and staging. Additionally, she earned the Graduate REALTOR® Institute (GRI) designation, Certified Professional Property Stager (PPS), Accredited Staging Professional (ASP), At Home With Diversity (AHWD) certification, GREEN Designation, Resort and Second-Home Property Specialist (RSPS), was a past member of the Master of Real Estate (MRE) Society, and continues ongoing training in relevant areas of real estate.

On a personal note: Laura shares her love of real estate with her best friend and husband of 22+ years, Greg, who is an owner with EZ Homes Inc., the largest wholesaler of foreclosed properties in the Valley and hard money lender. They have two wonderful sons, Gavin and Brayden, who enjoy Boy Scouts, video games, racing and just being boys! Laura's other interests include health and wellness (she is a certified Holistic Wellness Coach), family time, boating, beach time and spending time outdoors.

INSPIRED LIVING: YOUR HOME, OUR MISSION

LAURA JEWETT

My husband, Greg, and I embrace all aspects of real estate. Being in the real estate industry for over 21 years, we have spread our wings far and wide. Not only do we assist our clients in navigating the sale and/or purchase of their homes, but we also have a thriving business using our skills and knowledge to the fullest to create a legacy in both our business and our personal wealth goals.

We have in essence created our exit strategy from the beginning of our journey — long before we will actually leave the business (which may never happen!). We are uniquely positioned in the industry in that we have a construction division building new homes, remodel homes, own and operate numerous rental properties, and have a robust vacation rental portfolio. In addition, Greg has flipped thousands of acres of land, purchases properties at Trustee Sale (foreclosure properties) daily, and is a hard money lender. Having been in the industry for so long, we have always capitalized on the opportunities of the current market.

The best investment, without exception, is real estate! Real estate is a tax favored asset class, is a basic need that is always in demand, provides a hedge against inflation, has capital appreciation potential, and can produce CASH FLOW! No other asset class gives you all these benefits! So, our family legacy is to generate residual income beyond our own means for years or even generations to come. We walk the walk and talk the talk and this breeds confidence in our clients and business partners with whom we create this bigger vision every day.

As we continue to grow, we are building a team of three to four like-minded agents with administrative assistants. Being an independent brokerage is not essential, in our opinion, as our current broker is exceptional in providing support and training for their agents and teams. We also feel we can operate more efficiently using the systems and assets of a larger brokerage versus taking on these expenses independently.

Our business dealings, close partnerships, and service to our community positions us well to take the best care of our clients, which is at the heart of everything we do.

300 DAYS OF SUNSHINE

What makes Arizona special? Its diverse collection of people, who literally flock here from every corner of the US and beyond, are certainly a big part of it. And then there is the weather. Sure, we make headlines for our record breaking temps in the summer…quoting the catchphrase that we have so famously become known for, "It's a dry heat!" But as ridiculous as justifying 110+ degree temperatures may seem; this is a very true statement. We celebrate the remaining nine months of the year with blissful sun and fun filled days, matched with moderate temps and enough activities to fill the most active person's calendar. We are so fortunate to live, work, and play in a State that is so diverse in landscape and culture.

Some of my top favorites about living in this amazing state include:

1. Swimming to playing in the snow in two hours
2. 300 sunny days on average each year
3. Unbeatable sunsets and sunrises
4. Hiking and outdoor living year-round

5. No time changes!!
6. The Grand Canyon
7. Amazing Mexican food
8. A thriving sports and arts scene
9. Golf courses galore!
10. A navigable freeway and street system that makes our city easy to get around in

Being a 100% referral-based agent, I serve the greater Phoenix area, and having lived here my entire life I have a deep knowledge of the entire Valley. But having said that, Scottsdale, Paradise Valley, Cave Creek and Phoenix make up the bulk of our real estate dealings. Ironically, Covid had a significant positive impact on our real estate market. We witnessed an influx of people who were suddenly working remotely and wanted to move into the area because of the lifestyle that it affords; particularly people from high density cities like New York, Chicago, and Seattle who were looking for a spacious home with a private yard and pool. Our real estate market thrived during this challenging time and it was an honor to welcome so many new clients into our wonderful state!

GENERATIONAL REAL ESTATE

It was the summer before my graduating year in college when I first laid eyes on my future husband. It was literally love at first sight and I knew instantly that he was my 'person' with whom I wanted to spend the rest of my life. He was studying for his real estate license at the time, and I was completing my degrees in Marketing and Entrepreneurship while also beginning my career in sports marketing, working in event planning with the Fiesta Bowl. Simultaneously, I too decided right after graduation to get my license and never looked back.

Our two boys, 10 and 14 years old, are growing up in the industry and have plans to join our business as they mature. We are intent on nurturing their passions and dovetailing those into our business. Our eldest has an interest in technology and gadgets so wants to do drone photography for our listings. Our youngest likes to tour every house and has become a pro at pointing out all the "opportunities" in the house — which we have to remind him is not okay to do if the owners are around! LOL.

As with our family, our approach to our business is very much generational. We walk our clients through the whole process of not only home ownership but the journey beyond, one step at a time. The relationships we foster are what make us tick. Our desire to be there for our clients throughout their lifespans is really at the heart of our business.

SUPPORTING OUR CLIENTS AND COMMUNITY

Everything we do is in support of our clients and community. We have partnered with several local charities and host events throughout the year to not only celebrate our clients and foster our relationships with them but also to support these charity partners. For example, our popular annual movie night is always a fun-filled evening! We rent a movie theater — ideally on the opening night of a popular new feature — and invite our clients, strategic partners, and charities to enjoy a night of fun, networking and delicious snacks and prizes! The contributions we collect at these events on behalf of our charity partners is the best part! The generosity, love, and kindness that our tribe exhibits are humbling and inspiring!

These events provide a great opportunity to reach out to our client base and say, "Hey, how have you been? We would love for you to join us." This beats the typical phone call from agents saying, "Do you know anyone wanting to sell their home?" In addition to bringing a new level of fun into our business, this also keeps us top of mind with our 'tribe' that we have worked so hard to foster.

This idea comes from one of my favorite industry books, *7 Levels of Communication* by Michael J. Maher. Creating and maintaining good habits in my life and business is key to our success. Real estate is a full-time career and should be treated as such. This is a complex and constantly changing industry and staying educated and connected is imperative. Being available and a consistent source of accurate and relevant information to best support our client's real estate and life goals is paramount.

Having said this, it's a fine balance between setting personal limitations and ensuring your client's best interests are met. Developing a healthy work/life balance is a challenging yet essential necessity of being an entrepreneur and one that must constantly be monitored and honed. It is easy to forget that all business owners need regular office hours and time off to truly be effective, both for their clients and their families. Being somewhat of a workaholic, this is something I must consistently remind myself of.

Another crucial element of my life balance circle is dedicating time to be a leader in our community. I want to do more than just participate. I want to be a catalyst for change, a connector, and an influencer at every level.

Working with the team at Parkbench has helped us create strong ties within our community. Getting out and meeting new people and supporting their businesses is integral to this process . . . and it is fun! I thrive on being a connector within my circle of business alliances. For instance, I recently bridged a partnership between a local coffee shop and a custom candle business. Stark's Candle Company makes a coffee infused candle that would make your mouth water. So, I introduced the two towers, and now they are collaborating on making the coffee candles in branded coffee mugs!

Another example demonstrating how we merge and incorporate businesses is when I interviewed a catering company on Parkbench and now we use them to host many of our events throughout the year. In place of a client gift, we create a housewarming party at our clients' new house and invite their friends and new neighbors to participate. It's a great way to welcome them to the neighborhood and again foster community. Our families love having an opportunity to feel more connected to their neighborhood and as an added benefit, it also offers a great way to connect with neighbors who we then have the opportunity to cultivate relationships with.

CREATE HIGH LEVELS OF COMMUNICATION

With 21 years in this industry, I have certainly had my share of key learning moments along the way. One essential learning nugget stems from the old saying, *'One should work on their business and not just in it.'* One of the hardest and best things I ever did was hiring an assistant. When you are so used to doing everything yourself, it is sometimes hard to let go and let others participate in your business. Plus, finding someone who complements your strengths and weaknesses, mirrors your values, and who you enjoy being around, can be a complicated task!

Employing an assistant is an essential step to grow and turn real estate from merely a job into a flourishing business. I had so many great ideas for how I wanted my business to run and how I wanted to serve my clients and community, but until I was able to free myself from the daily tasks required to keep the wheels turning, I was unable to effectively implement them. I took the next step of getting my assistant licensed, which opens growth opportunities for her as well as provides me with a trusted partner who can assist clients when I am unavailable . . . thus enhancing my work/life balance opportunities.

Database. Database. Database. Sure, location is the primary factor when buying or selling a home, but your database is the equivalent to this in terms of running an effective business, especially if you are relationship-based. Keeping your CRM up to date, with detailed and meaningful notes on your contacts, including knowing who their family members are and what's important to their lives is critical. Having and continually enhancing this information through consistent and meaningful contact will create a higher level of communication between you and your current and future clients, strategic partners, and business associates.

Handwritten notes are a dying art and that's precisely why we do them. They differentiate us from the crowd and digital noise and provide a personal touch, which is far more impactful than an email or text. Think about the last time you received a handwritten note in the mail and how it made you feel. In this digital age, it is a nice feeling knowing someone cares enough to take the time to do this. Staying focused and remaining consistent with the people in your database is the key to creating a referral-based business of people who know, like and trust you!

INSPIRED LIVING

Inspiration is literally built into our business. InspiredLivingCollective.com is more than a brand, it's a lifestyle. By definition, inspire means to 'breathe life into or to fill someone with the urge or ability to do or feel something' (*Oxford Languages*). We are the Inspired Living Real Estate Collective, a division of Platinum Living Realty. Our name conveys our team mission to provide the tools for our clients to find inspiration throughout their entire homeownership journey as well as their lives beyond the transaction. Real estate is such a wonderfully diverse industry! I am challenged and intrigued daily by something new — and I love this! And I love real estate; that is to say, houses! And I truly love connecting people with the perfect home for the next chapter in their lives. I love earning clients' trust and having them share their very personal family goals and aspirations with me, sharing in their excitement about what we are working on together and inviting me to be part of their major decision-making moments. A home is a story of who we are and a collection of the things we love. Being a partner and an advocate to help my clients achieve this goal is my privilege.

Perspective is EVERYTHING! Challenges are truly opportunities to learn and grow. I have been very successful at cycling past 'problems' and thinking creatively to find solutions instead. Nearly every real estate transaction brings at least a few surprises or challenges and having the level headedness to think through all the variables and find effective solutions is what will set you apart and make you a hero for your clients.

My other passions are holistic nutrition and healthy living. What you put into your body (including food and information) is vitally important to your health and wellbeing . . . 'garbage in, garbage out!'

Your home and your health are part of your journey through life and weaving my lifestyle into my business just comes naturally.

MY WHY

What comes to mind when I am asked about why I do what I do is, in part, wanting to create something much larger than myself and create a legacy that lives beyond my years. My goal over the next 10 years is to create and cultivate a small team of agents who see the vision of giving back and building a business based on love, generosity, and appreciation! At that stage, I want to step into more of an advisory role for my clients and agents as opposed to working the daily tasks that my team can manage without me. This will allow me to spend more time with my family and enjoy some more of the beach lifestyle I crave!

The second half of my why is being a connector in my community. Using the techniques that Parkbench offers, as well as capitalizing on my business knowledge, provides the opportunities for me to support and promote other local small businesses and charity organizations that make our community the amazing place it is!

GIVING A HELPING HAND

Working with and supporting local non-profit organizations is near and dear to my heart. I was raised with an awareness of the needs of others around me and the importance of stepping in to make a difference in people's lives. In adulthood, my charitable giving journey began with a poster that caught my eye. While I was waiting to meet a client at Starbucks, I was perusing the bulletin board where I came across a poster that was recruiting volunteers to make a difference in children's lives through the foster care system. It wasn't a special post, but it spoke to me. I couldn't let it go. A few days later I filled out the application, completed the fingerprint and background clearances, and became a state-appointed Foster Care Review Board (FCRB) member. We interview all the interested parties in foster cases and put forth recommendations to the assigned judge based on our findings. It is truly an incredible blend of heart-breaking and heart-warming work, and an amazing experience that I am so proud to be a part of. It is truly my honor to be the voice and an advocate for these children, who oftentimes don't have one.

The Inspired Living Real Estate Collective is committed to giving back in our own backyard! Our strategic philanthropic program called OPERATION GIVE BACK focuses on four core areas: Children, Health, Homelessness and Animals. A portion of every commission we earn is contributed to one of these local charities on behalf of our clients. As noted previously, we also host contribution drives throughout the year to collect essential items for these amazing organizations. We are honored to serve these incredible organizations and support their missions to make our communities better, stronger and more connected! We cheerfully contribute to create community!

Our first charity partner was *Arizona Helping Hands,* which was a natural extension of my work as an FCRB Board Member. They collect needed essentials as well as items that bring joy and a smile to foster kids' faces, which are then provided to foster families. Their vision is simple: 'Every child in foster care is safe and loved.'

Maggie's Place is amazing! They support homeless women who are pregnant. Logically, it makes sense to help women be successful parents to prevent their children from ever having to enter the foster system. "Maggie's Place welcomes pregnant and parenting women and their children into a safe and loving community, providing life-changing programs and ongoing services to help them to become self-sufficient."

The *Arizona Pet Project* helps keep pets with their families who are facing hard times. They are different from any other pet organization out there. By keeping pets with their families, it helps lessen the trauma that families are already enduring as well as keeps these beloved animals out of shelters and possible euthanasia. "Our unique approach and revolutionary programs are focused on improving and saving the lives of both people and pets by keeping pets with the families who love them."

The *Joy Bus Diner* provides healthy meals to cancer patients who are fighting cancer alone. Volunteers deliver the meals and stay and provide companionship and conversation. These connections are vital for these people who otherwise may have no one. I lost my mom to cancer when I was 20 and the impact of that has never left my soul. Supporting others who are fighting this battle is incredibly important to me, knowing all the pain and challenges it brings. "Our sole purpose is to relieve the daily struggles of people with cancer by delivering a fresh and healthy meal with a friendly face."

All of these organizations are run by some of the most amazing people that I have ever met and while I chose them, I really feel like they found me. It is an honor to support them in their inspiring missions! If everyone aligned themselves with a cause that is meaningful to them, think of the change we could create in the world!

A FEW LAST WORDS

As I step into my 22nd year of service I reflect upon the countless clients, friends, family members, business associates, and charity partners who have been by my side encouraging and supporting me every step of the way. I want to thank my incredibly dedicated and loving partner and husband, Greg, who is my biggest fan and an amazing father to our two boys, Gavin and Brayden…who are the loves of my life and my biggest why!

Like many success stories, I have my parents to thank for instilling in me a solid work ethic, an open awareness of the needs of those around me, and a solid foundation built on doing the right thing, always. My dad would consistently tell us that anything worth doing is worth doing well. Of course, as a child this message was not always well received as it often meant we had not completed a chore or task to the best of our ability, and it would need to be redone . . . but eventually I realized this was a mantra worth living by. My mom led by example and was the purest demonstrator of what it means to be a dedicated and committed person. She was a true inspiration of strength, ambition, and unconditional love, even amid insurmountable odds. She was my rock! Thank you, mom and dad! And of course, I cannot forget my sister who is also my best friend. Thank you for always having a joyful heart and being up for any adventure!

As I close this chapter, I am forever grateful for having a career I love with a mission to serve and to leave a lasting impression on my community!

Laura Jewett

REACH OUT TO LAURA JEWETT

Platinum Living Realty
Cell: 480.628.2563
Office: 480.563.7963
Laura@AZInspiredLiving.com
www.InspiredLivingCollective.com

WHAT CLIENTS ARE SAYING ABOUT LAURA

> *"I have been in real estate for almost 20 years in California, I can tell you first hand that I have never dealt with someone in the business that actually genuinely cares for her clients. Laura understands how to close a deal and make her clients happy. We would not have the house we have today if it were not for her. Stop wasting your time with other agents and work with someone that gets it. Coming from someone in commercial real estate and dealing with other agents selling homes, best advice I can give."*

~ Keith & Heather B.

"Laura is absolutely amazing! She is extremely skilled at negotiating and navigating through very tense and difficult situations. Our listing was extremely challenging, but Laura always remained calm, cool and collected. She is very even keeled and keeps the emotion out of the transaction. When experience and professionalism matter, you need the best on your team. We are especially grateful to have Laura represent us. We highly recommend her!"

~ Daryl Z.

"I just wanted to let you know how much we appreciate your honesty and integrity. There are few like you in the world. Thanks Laura, we appreciate all you do."

~Jim R.

"Regardless of the size of our next purchase I wouldn't think of using another agent. Laura has such a great grasp of how to represent her clients that you never doubt if she is doing everything possible. We always feel that we are still well represented and supported even after the sale. I can't begin to name all the instances in which she has gone above and beyond in serving our family."

~Jim H.

CHAPTER 5
BEYOND BROCHURES

"I BELIEVE IN MAKING A DIFFERENCE BECAUSE SOMEONE ONCE BELIEVED IN ME!"

DIANE RATZLAFF
CASTLE ROCK, CO

GET TO KNOW DIANE RATZLAFF

I am a Real Estate Agent who has been in the housing industry in different capacities for decades. I started out as an assistant/transaction coordinator to some extraordinarily successful real estate agents and was able to experience a large volume of business at a quick pace. From there, I went into the mortgage world where I became a loan file manager for a fortune 500 company. In 2020 I became a licensed Loan Originator, expanding my knowledge of the loan process. So now, not only do I have a thorough understanding of the real estate business, I also understand the intricacies of the mortgage industry. As a licensed agent, it is my goal to do a phenomenal job for my clients. Trust in a relationship is earned, therefore, it is my goal to diligently aim higher than expected and deliver an exceptional experience to my clients.

BEYOND BROCHURES

DIANE RATZLAFF

6224 FEET ABOVE SEA LEVEL

As a native to Colorado, I consider myself so blessed to live amongst the rolling hills and small-town charm of Castle Rock. The first settlers came to this region in search of striking it rich with gold, and with land which was available through the Homestead Act of 1864. Today, Castle Rock is one of the fastest growing communities and Douglas County is ranked as the fourth wealthiest county in the nation!

Situated at 6224 feet above sea level and along the front range of the Rocky Mountains, Castle Rock boasts jaw-dropping scenery, miles and miles of hiking and biking trails, and 300 days of sunshine throughout the year! Castle Rock's proximity to Denver, the clean environment, and natural beauty of the Colorado foothills make our town an attractive residential community. With all this to offer, it's no wonder Castle Rock enjoys a robust real estate market.

One of my favorite festivities is the starlighting event which takes place every Thanksgiving. People gather near the city center and enjoy ice skating, music, and local fare. Once the fireworks start, I feel the magic of this quaint town — my town.

CHANGES IN THE MARKET

As of late, the inventory has been up in terms of housing listings, but they are staying on the market a little longer than what we have witnessed in the last two years. As the interest rates continue to climb, the environment is settling out a bit.

Colorado is considered a 'purple' state which means our Governor is Democratic but most of the outlying counties are mainly Republican. People come here because they want a more conservative and traditional living environment. For example, during the COVID-19 pandemic, many people moved here because they didn't want to wear masks mandated in their home states.

From highrise condos (six stories) to spread-out, sprawling acreages, we have a huge assortment of lifestyle living options. Our downtown core attracts all sorts. It has local breweries, mom-and-pop restaurants, and warm and welcoming neighborhood pubs. One does not have to go to Denver to experience downtown living, we have it all here.

We have had a large influx of people from California, Texas, and New York. This is due in part to people seeking a four-season climate and the lifestyle that comes with it. One can ski, snowboard, snowmobile, snowshoe, in the winter and then kayak, fish, and hike in the warmer months. Because of the countless outdoor activities, people tend to be more health-conscious and seek active adventures.

POLAROID PICTURES

Real estate picked me! In 1987 I was a flight attendant with United Airlines. It wasn't quite paying the bills, so I was looking for a side hustle. I happened upon a job in a real estate firm where I oversaw the marketing brochures. I went to houses to measure the square footage and write the descriptions about them.

To give perspective, this was before the advent of computers and phones with cameras in them.

I would attach the polaroid pictures to the sheets and photocopy them for distribution. Times have changed.

In 1992 I got married to my husband who owned a property preservation company that dealt with foreclosures and evictions. I was responsible for the accounting and processing side of the business. That same year, Hurricane Andrew struck, and the business took him to Florida and the southern states, where he was working with an investor fixing and reselling houses.

This experience left him wanting to be inside an air-conditioned BMW like the other real estate agents he was meeting. He got his license while I was pregnant with our first child, so I was a little anxious, not knowing how we were going to make ends meet. I stepped into this new business as an unlicensed assistant, showing houses and keeping the books in order.

2010 rolled around when we decided to separate and take on new lives. I worked for another Realtor® who also did property preservation. I was the one who had to tell people they needed to leave their homes. These were often moms whose husbands hadn't told them they were behind in their mortgage payments and their homes were foreclosing. It was heart-breaking.

I later worked as a loan officer's assistant and found myself dealing with a lot of real estate agents. I was so frustrated by the lack of professionalism from these agents that I thought to myself, "I can do better."

STARTING FROM ZERO

I entered my new career with guarded enthusiasm as I did not have a sphere of influence of any sort, and I was working from scratch. In my first year I closed 12 deals, but I felt I wasn't doing very well so I panicked. I answered an ad for a transaction coordinator at another realty office. I interviewed with the head of the team, and she promptly told me that she wouldn't hire me.

Of course, I was devastated and tried to hold my tears back until she said, "But I will have you come on as an agent." I was grappling with the idea, but she assured me they would help out in any way, and they did. They gave me a lead right away, but it wasn't going to be easy. The client had a difficult time getting mortgage approval, but I managed to get it under contract and have a successful outcome. I spent five years with this boutique firm, BTT, and established my database and sphere of influence. I am eternally grateful to them.

Just before the pandemic hit, I wanted to spread my wings, so I moved over to Keller-Williams. Little did I know, everything would be shut down and the game changed significantly. At that time, we had to present an offer before we even stepped into the property. I was again in the position of selling only 12 houses that year.

I had to pivot quickly so I joined another team, The Metro 5280 Home Team. Earlier this year, we moved to Fathom Realty® as a team, in response to my intuition. The mentoring program here is exceptional and I'm glad to be part of this aspect of the business. The mandate in this office is to help new agents create sustainable businesses. We are also rewarded with stock options for bringing people in, but this isn't my driving force. I'm a certified mentor with Fathom and I love the role I'm involved in because I want to 'build' better real estate agents, one at a time!

Being a mentor to others can only help me be a better agent as well. I know that going back to the basics and relearning some elements can only help my endgame. I'm in a much better position now to be of service to others.

I'm not one to let grass grow under me, so during the pandemic I obtained my Loan Originator license. I believe this diversification allows me to ride out the ebbs and flows of the real estate world. It also makes me a better real estate agent because I know the back end of the finance world, which allows me to advise my clients at a higher level.

MEETING THE LOCALS

I've been involved in both past and present volunteer organizations and charities. I used to actively partake in the local community garden projects, Girl Scouts, and the Elizabeth Stampede Rodeo. I learned a lot from my interactions with various people and I met so many new people who are now part of my life. I currently make meals for my church group which service the local membership.

I am a member of the Colorado Women's Council of Realtors®. I'm a mentor for Fathom, and it is this work that I really enjoy because I can be of service to other agents and help them be better — again, one at a time.

I believe in making a difference because someone once believed in me!

CHANGING TRAJECTORY

Nothing changes one's life trajectory quite like divorce does and mine was no exception. I basically had to start from scratch and go out on my own with few resources other than my self-determination. But if I can be an example of getting through to the other side, then I'm happy to offer guidance.

"I can do this" was my mantra that got me through the tough times. Dealing with the divorce and starting my career with two children at home, was no easy feat but I have to say that the love and support I received from Brian and Lee at BTT Real Estate was integral to me continuing along my real estate path.

I will say this, because I worked with my husband all those years, I do owe a debt of gratitude to him as our arrangement allowed me to be there as my children grew up. Scratched knees, first goals, and report cards were the center of my world and there is no greater honor than being a mom. You are my 'why' and Delta Dawn still plays in the background of our lives.

WOULD YOU HIRE YOU?

What does it take to be a successful agent?

- 40+ hours a week, to begin with.
- Become a local expert.
- Be educated.
- Own a business, not a job.
- Be personal with people.
- Get up every day and be on purpose.
- Have a plan.
- Hire an assistant.

- Always ask people, "What can I do for you?"
- Continue to learn.
- Communicate. Communicate. Communicate!

Lastly, ask yourself, "Would you hire you?" If the answer is no, then there is some work to be done. If the answer is yes, then keep going and keep improving.

STAYING IN TOUCH

I can't say enough about keeping you and your brand top of mind with your database and key influencers. For instance, I network with other agents as I often get referrals from them. I send several handwritten notes throughout the year, often piggy backing on fun holidays when they don't expect it. On St Paddy's Day I send out a lottery ticket with a note saying, 'I'm lucky you are my client.'

I also try to keep up to date with my clients' family lives, in particular their birthdays or their children's milestones, like graduations. At Thanksgiving time, our office hands out pumpkin and apple pies to our 'A' client list. People happily stop by and chat with us about their plans for the holiday. Once again, this is a unique way of touching base with people.

My brand is one set at a very personal level. The fact that a client is going to entrust me with the most important investment of their lives, is taken very seriously and I don't want to mess it up. I have to get to a fundamentally intimate place with people to gain their trust. A fun example of this is when I was invited to my client's new home and to celebrate, we shotgunned beer! That's right, I shotgunned a beer with these people — and enjoyed every minute of it!

GETTING OUT OF MY OWN WAY

Part of the reason I joined on with Parkbench is to get me out of my comfort zone. By this I mean I get very nervous in front of the camera and then meeting new people makes it even more terrifying. I've created a few videos now for posting and I am getting cautiously more confident. I preach about getting out of your own way, so I had better take my own medicine!

As a matter of fact, my very first interview was at a winery and well, I think I was over-served. LOL. The tastings were so good, and they kept serving, so I kept going. Needless to say, I bought a case of their wine upon finishing up.

The accountability to my new website platform helps me stay on top of my game and not just a player on the sidelines.

SO THANKFUL

I want to thank my ex-husband, again, for helping me with my real estate journey. I fell in love with real estate when I worked with you.

Brian and Lee of BTT Realty breathed life into my career when I thought I couldn't move forward. Thank you both!

My team at Fathom Realty, Metro 5280 Home Team, thank you so much for believing in me and elevating my presence in my community.

Thank you to my kids and family for putting up with me all these years. To my daughter, Tanya, thank you for the constant encouragement and support and the notes you leave around the house, "I love you mama, you're killing it!" My son, Colby, I wish you all the best as you embark on your own career as a real estate agent. You both make me proud.

Diane Ratzlaff

REACH OUT TO DIANE RATZLAFF

Broker Associate
720-891-7444 (Phone/Text)
Fathom Realty Colorado
Diane5280re@gmail.com

WHAT CLIENTS ARE SAYING ABOUT DIANE

"Diane was very informative on the area and units we were looking at as well as great tips to make sure that not only was I going to move to something I really liked but would also be in the best shape. She goes above and beyond even after the purchase is complete to make sure getting settled in is as smooth as possible."

~Ancar S.

"Diane is one of the best Real Estate Professionals I have ever worked with. She and I worked together with Clients that had very specific needs and she was able to get them under contract within a very short amount of time. She is knowledgeable and very fun to work with. I would recommend her to anyone looking to buy or sell a home!"

~Dianna G.

"I used Diane to move from our starter home in Aurora. We got her through a builder looking at new homes. She definitely helped me out with my nerves in moving. She's got the best communication skills and is realistic with her approach. Diane always had my back and told me what I needed to hear, not what I always wanted to hear. During the process I wasn't sure about anything, the decision I made deciding to move on from our starter home of 15 years, such huge decisions in life, but after everything was finished, I was happy I found Diane. I'd definitely use her again. She's a great person who cares about her clients, is realistic and is an excellent communicator."

~Patchwork Brewing

CHAPTER 6

E KOMO MAI (WELCOME TO MY HOME)

"I HAVE A REPUTATION OF GETTING THINGS DONE AND I LIKE TO THINK THIS IS WHY OTHER REAL ESTATE AGENTS LIKE TO WORK WITH ME. THEY KNOW WHAT THEY ARE GOING TO GET. I AM A FIRM BELIEVER THAT AGENTS SHOULD VIEW EACH OTHER AS RUNNING MATES AND NOT COMPETITION."

CINDY RASMUSSEN
HONOLULU, HI

GET TO KNOW CINDY RASMUSSEN

As an agent who's an expert in the Makiki/Manoa, Honolulu local area, Cindy brings her wealth of knowledge and expertise about buying and selling real estate so that she can be most helpful to you. It's not the same everywhere, so you need someone you can trust for up-to-date information. Cindy lives to help you find your next dream home.

Cindy Rasmussen has earned the designations of BPOR, GRI, and SRS. She has invested time in educating herself so that she can be most valuable to you by being capable of taking care of all of your real estate needs. When she is not working to serve her real estate clients, you might find her tending orchids in her garden, playing ukulele with friends and family, or testing out another restaurant in her neighborhood.

Cindy was born and raised in Hawaii. During the school years, she lived on the island of Oahu where she attended grade school through high school. When she was not in school, she spent most of her time on the island of Hawaii, aka the Big Island, the island of her family's origin. She says that summers at Gram's house were the best of times. They lived in Kona, in a small town known as Holualoa. Grandpa was a cowboy at Greenwell Ranch. While Grandpa was at work, she helped Gram tend to the many animals (Chickens, pigs, dogs, and rabbits) and picked coffee that they grew on their property. Although this might sound like hard work, to a child, this was heavenly! She could not enjoy this much fun in the city.

Her parents worked hard to provide Cindy and her brother with private school educations. Because her parents worked so much, Cindy looked forward to those vacations when the whole family (and the dog) would head to Kona to spend time with Gram and Grandpa. What a life!

Cindy maintains relationships in the same fashion that she was raised, in a simple country way, where people say what they mean and a handshake is as binding as any contract.

E KOMO MAI (WELCOME TO MY HOME)

CINDY RASMUSSEN

ALOHA

Imagine waking up every day to the sound of the ocean waves and birds chirping in your backyard. Or imagine experiencing jaw-dropping rainbows every day in the valley and then realizing that the pot at the end of the rainbow is your home. Aloha and welcome to my home of Makiki/Manoa, Hawaii.

Makiki/Manoa is rich in history and has the bragging rights of some of the largest and oldest residential lots on the island of Oahu. Posh neighborhoods are common here and so they attract people who seek a more secluded lifestyle with sprawling houses and gardens. Manoa is set in a lush valley with countless hiking trails, like the rocky rainforest trail to the popular Manoa Falls.

The University of Hawaii is located in Manoa and is known as a major teaching and research facility. Competitive sports is at the heart of the University with beach volleyball, golf and football amongst the more popular teams. On another level surfing, paddleboarding, canoeing and pickleball are year-round sports that all can enjoy.

"THE VALLEY OF THE RAINBOWS"

For the last 5 or so years most of my business has been from out of state relocations. The typical story of folks getting married here or a military couple being stationed here then dreaming of the day they can come back as permanent residents. Some relocations include those who once lived here, then left for college elsewhere. Life kept them away, and now they finally come back. Manoa is not for the faint of 'wallet' as it takes quite a bit of money to afford living in this paradise!

A modest cottage home in Manoa may easily exceed 1 million dollars but that is quite normal for most parts of the islands. A shanty on a green lot can be upwards of 2-3 million dollars-easy. Having said this, Manoa is one of the most beautiful places in the world, with sizable lots that are rare indeed.

The weather is gorgeous year-round and we often wake up to morning dew or light rain in the valley. And what does rain bring along with it? Rainbows! On occasion, 2-3 rainbows can be seen at the same time while we enjoy warm tradewinds gently blowing along the Manoa valley.

I think we are totally spoiled here, yet we don't realize it. Let me explain. In this region the sun is always on our backs, even when it's raining. We call this liquid sunshine. We certainly have a lot to complain about, you know. The weather is pretty consistent, generally temperatures are in the 80's for most of the day. When we get cold, it can get as low as 70 or 72 degrees. Now that's cold, right? Yes, we complain about these 'horrific' conditions that others would kill for, but that's part of the island life charm!

WE SUFFERED LESS

During the last recession and inflation hike, the islands really did suffer less in terms of escalating costs and lower house market prices in comparison to the rest of mainland U.S.A. This was due in large part to the land mass being so small and the demand being so high. We typically have limited inventory but a higher amount of buyers wanting in.

These last two years (2020/21) we all experienced a very active market across North America. For example, one of my listings recently received about 15 offers, before the ink dried! (On some days, I confess that I wished I had an unlisted phone number!)) The federal government has introduced interest rate hikes to combat inflation and the inflated prices of housing. It appears that this has helped to slow down the 'crazy' buying frenzy a little. With a most recent offer on behalf of my buyers, ours was one of eight offers. (At least we didn't have to compete with 15 others this time.) . Happy ending, our offer was accepted. My buyers will soon become new homeowners.

MY $99.00 START INTO REAL ESTATE

I got into real estate by accident. It was the early 1990s when I separated from my husband and had to create a new life for myself and daughter. I wanted to get a place for us but I didn't know where to begin. Too proud to ask for help, I managed to find a course that prequalified me to get my license. Can you believe the price for the entire course was only $99? Of course I had no intention of obtaining a license, I just wanted the knowledge to help me buy my own place.

My instructor encouraged me to take the final exam and get my license as she thought I would be good in the business. She also suggested I hang my hat in her brokerage and the rest is history!

I got my feet wet with property management and my mom, who was also licensed at the time, was a big help. She was licensed on the Big Island and so moved her license to Oahu to help support me and set me up. Shortly after, I 'stumbled' on my first listing when a friend reached out to me and asked for my expertise. That very first transaction was well over a million dollars. Luckily we live in Hawaii!

GO VOTE!

My father was from Denmark and came to the United States after he was recruited into the U.S. Army. The promise was if he served time, the government would help him become an American citizen. Oddly enough, he never became a citizen until more than fifty years later. I can still remember my mom sending in his 'alien' status card every year in order to remain on American soil.

Growing up my father insisted we learn and speak English because we were American, even though he remained a Dane for most of my life. Fast forward-my father woke me up one election day and told me to go vote! This would have been my first experience at voting, but I didn't see why it was that important. He set me straight on that. "The polls are open and you have to vote because it is a privilege and right in this country."

His sense of duty didn't stop there. He taught us that we should support local and buy local in order to keep the economy going in our community. This was the groundwork that set me up to be community-minded and support my neighbors to this day.

I enjoy getting involved in local initiatives. My favorite volunteer job is working with a group called Soroptimist International of the Americas. Meaning, "Best for Women," Soroptimist is a global organization that provides women and girls with access to the education and training they need to achieve economic empowerment and live their dreams!

Once again, I got involved in this organization by 'accident.' A client/friend of mine invited me for lunch to one of their meetings and she sat me down at the reception table and put me to work! She insisted on me joining the group and even said she would pay for my membership, but that wasn't necessary. I joined right away as I saw the huge value that this group offered.

The charter of our group at that time was that you had to be in business and there wouldn't be any overlap of industries. This was set up as an aside to the overall function of the charity, to which I was very grateful. I guess the premise is if we are successful then we can help others to be the same.

LIST OR SELL?

The whole concept of Parkbench and its platform, really coincides with my belief system and values. I believe people should learn about their communities and support the small businesses when and where they can.

As for business, I am meeting all sorts of interesting people and making lots of new connections. I interviewed a baker who owns 5 bakeries and somehow survived the Pandemic lockdowns, which strained most businesses. Can you believe that this same business owner actually opened up another business during the pandemic? (Now that's a community leader!) I also interviewed a bike shop owner who was the 4th generation family member to run the shop. There is no shortage of incredible business owners in my neighborhood. It's just one of the things I love about my neighborhood.

My concept is to launch my interview/video platform- "Meet Your Neighbors" as a way to drive business to them.

My very first listing was through someone I knew, so I understand the importance of having a sphere of influence. Although I didn't rely on family and close friends to help me get started I do get help from them from time to time.

That first sale was a million dollar listing which I thought I priced competitively; although it was higher than all the other homes on the market at that time It really was a beautiful home. I hosted an open house and the local Realtors® came by only to tell me that I was over pricing the house and I would never get what was being asked. Well, as it turned out, we got over listing and this set the tone for future listings in the area to follow suit.

There are agents who will try to push price over value, but I refuse to play that game. Part of my philosophy when listing is- "Do you want to simply list or do you want to sell your property?" I want to work together or not at all. I'm a brutally honest and transparent person and I believe that's why people like working with me.

I have a reputation of getting things done and I like to think this is why other real estate agents like to work with me. They know what they are going to get. I am a firm believer that agents should view each other as running mates and not competition. Another example is I offer the other agents a chance to look at escrow contracts in the event of contingency. They are usually shocked by this but I have nothing to hide. When we both focus on the common goal of helping our respective clients achieve their dreams, the outcome is always rewarding.

MECHANICAL MIND-SET

As a new agent, my mind-set was quite mechanical as I didn't take into account the numerous factors involved in pricing a home. (Heck, what did I know as a newbie?) I was primed with a family background in a commercial industry so my approach back then was to treat residential listings in the same manner as commercial. So I went about business as usual and I priced my first listing based on square footage calculations. It's no wonder those agents thought I was out to lunch! Today, I am thankful for all the 'mistakes' and challenges that I overcame and I now have my recipe for success.

If I can offer one piece of advice it is this: If you are a new agent starting out, ask a lot of questions of your clients and listen to their answers! I get so much value from my clients and this truly helps me be a better agent.

Some dos and don'ts of advice I wish I took when I started out:

- Be polite-all the time.
- Be respectful- all the time.
- Always smile.
- Be genuine, friendly and caring.
- Don't hide.
- Don't be afraid.
- Never assume your client knows what you know.
- Don't use acronyms like MLS because people may not understand them.

I like to help people beyond their own expectations of me. For instance, because I am a firm believer in educating my clients as much as possible, I sometimes give my clients a copy of my book, "Selling Secrets You Can't Afford to Miss."

ENJOY EVERY OPPORTUNITY

I want to thank both Betty and Frank Dower who were my first brokers. Betty was also the instructor who encouraged me to start my real estate business. They taught me to be of service to anyone I came in contact with and they both never missed a moment to be grateful. It was very much like the values my parents instilled in me from the beginning.This advice has served me well.

I take every opportunity possible to learn from experiences. I live in gratitude every day and I love what I do. I can still hear my Grandfather in the back of my head; "Always do a good job the best way you know how and make it easy for the next guy." Hey Grandpa, I'm doing it!!

Cindy Rasmussen

REACH OUT TO CINDY RASMUSSEN

Phone: (808) 478-4781
Email: CindyHomefinder@gmail.com
Office: 94-1024 Waipio Uka Street, Suite #206 Waipahu, HI 96797
Website: https://www.HonoluluAreaHomefinder.com

WHAT CLIENTS ARE SAYING ABOUT CINDY

"Cindy is very easy to work with and kept in touch the entire time!"

~ Cooperating Agent

"Yes, she was very professional, and helpful!"

~ Alex S.

"Thank you Cindy for a smooth transaction!"

~Eric Y.

"Cindy is a joy to work with. Her positive outlook and her authentic win-win attitude made the transaction seamless. I would love to work with Cindy again!"

~ Tracy B.

CHAPTER 7

ENTREPRENEUR FROM THE START

"Our motto is "Do what you say you're going to do and when you say you are going to do it." This helps us keep our focus and firmly plants honesty and integrity into everything we do."

Cris Kambouris
Windsor-Essex, ON

GET TO KNOW CRIS KAMBOURIS

Cris is a leading real estate representative and multiple award-winning and top-producing listing agent. Cris is the first Windsor agent at Keller Williams Lifestyles Realty, and he has a vast knowledge base in all aspects of residential, commercial, investment real estate and development. He has sold countless homes all over the Windsor-Essex area, including Southlawn Gardens, Southwood Lakes, Roseland Golf Course area, Riverside, St. Mary's Gate, Historic Walkerville area, Tecumseh, Lakeshore, LaSalle and much more.

These Windsor and surrounding communities offer a beautiful selection of condominiums, waterfront properties, modern and historic homes, for sale or lease. Cris is a senior accredited listing agent who often accompanies many out of town buyers looking to relocate or retire in popular and trending Windsor-Essex locations.

When Cris is not showing a property, you will find him involved with many Windsor and LaSalle community projects. Connection with the Windsor-Essex community and networking with local business owners plays a crucial role in his success.

Cris has developed a simple, transparent, and easy to understand process for his buyers and sellers.

ENTREPRENEUR FROM THE START

CRIS KAMBOURIS

Windsor-Essex is one of the most dynamic and unique cities in Canada due, in part, to the influx of various people from across our country into our city. It is a real hub in the Greater Toronto area as it sits along the U.S. border state of Michigan. As a border town, we have a lot of professionals, like nurses and engineers, that work in Detroit and commute back and forth. Having said this, Windsor is also attractive to many retirees as the cost of living is lower and the access to Florida and Arizona as their second homes is convenient and affordable.

People who live in South Windsor have very strong loyalties to their community and for good reason. This area boasts some of the best schools in the country, including St. Clair College and the University of Windsor are known well for their Business and Law programs as well as the nursing faculty.

As far as the housing market is concerned, there are numerous single-family, townhomes, semi-detached houses and condominium complexes, offering a mix for individual tastes. More specifically, an area known as Kingsville is home to many wineries and hosts countless real estate investment properties in the form of Airbnbs. One very unique development on the nearby Boblo Island is the gentrification of an old amusement park into new neighbourhoods. Beautiful homes, parks and marinas are just a few of the attractions one can find here.

My business this year comprised of 26% of out-of-town residents buying locally and I expect this number to rise over the next couple of years. This is due largely to the 4.8 billion dollar mega battery plant being built here for alternative-powered vehicles. The joint venture is between automobile maker Stellantis and LG Energy Solution from South Korea. Upwards of 2500 jobs will be created which is a relief to this area hard-hit by the layoffs in the traditional auto industry.

JUST POPPING BY

I love working and living in my area of South Windsor. It is vibrant with young couples moving in, remodeling homes and raising their families. We support numerous restaurants, pubs and hardware stores, to name a few, by sponsoring events that will attract people to the area. Our sports teams also attract a lot of attention and as a husband and father of three kids, I am always lending a helping hand.

As an ambassador for the Canadian Mental Health Association and sponsor of "Fantastic Fathers" I keep involved at the grassroots level. "Fantastic Fathers" is an organization created to support divorced and single fathers and their children through some difficult times.

During the Covid pandemic, my team and I were involved in handing out Covid safety kits to all our clients and throughout our community. It wasn't soon after I got involved, I realized that many establishments were managing an almost impossible situation and were under a lot of pressure. So my team and I ordered pizzas for all of the employees at numerous businesses in the community.

As we like to tie in fun into our everyday business activities, we give away pumpkin pies to our 'A' and 'B' clients. Who doesn't love pie? If pie isn't enough, we give our clients a basket of goodies including popcorn, pop and chocolate bars and call it, "Just popping by."

We often help out when a family is in dire need, in our community. We write them a cheque and donate on the spot. It's that simple. We just want to give.

SINCE I WAS 15 YEARS OLD

My real estate career began in 2005, but my life as an entrepreneur started when I was 15 years old. By the time I was 24 years old, I owned 6 restaurants and bars, in which I leveraged my knowledge gained from my Business and Finance degrees from the University of Windsor. I also invested in real estate and even wrote my own leases for my commercial properties. Everyone kept asking me to become a real estate agent because I knew so much about it and I studied all aspects from construction of buildings to contract preparation.

So I got my real estate license! Because my restaurants were so successful and I was young I figured that I would work the business part-time. Then when things got so busy with my 'new' business I had some decisions to make. I knew in my heart though that real estate was IT for me so I started the process of selling off my restaurants and taking on more and more clients.

Fast forward to today, my team and I are grateful to have an 85% referral business and I attribute this to the hard work, dedication and customer service we provide our clients.

OUR GROWING TEAM

As any team grows and expands it's important to hire the right people for the right job. In our case, it was important to hire assistants to help with the daily intake and our increasing social media presence. Our full time social media person keeps our brand in the forefront of people's minds and our brand relevant and fresh. My son, Evan has also recently joined our small team and he is a master at video production and drone photography.

One of our goals has always been to work closely with local businesses and support them anyway we can. Working with Parkbench allows us to weave our video interviews and sponsorships into one nice, tight platform. We look forward to elevating our causes beyond what we can do alone.

Our motto is "Do what you say you're going to do and when you say you are going to do it." This helps us keep our focus and firmly plants honesty and integrity into everything we do.

HIT THE CEILING

Before I joined Keller-Williams Realty, I was an independent agent with an assistant at my previous brokerage. I hit a ceiling but didn't know how to grow. My turning point happened when I attended the "Family Reunion" event that Keller-Williams hosted every year. I became the first agent in Windsor-Essex to join Keller-Williams and I have nothing but praise for them.

I have taken over 50 seminars with them in the last 3 years and I have learned more during this time than the previous 14 years!

One day, every year, ALL Keller-Williams agents participate in "Red Day" where we show up with a 'servant's heart', roll up our sleeves and help local schools and food banks. In addition to their philanthropic actions, the teamwork across offices is exceptional. I can step into any KW office, anywhere and feel welcomed by their sharing and collaboration efforts.

CHALLENGE ACCEPTED

The market back in 2005 wasn't what I would call good. It was in fact 'tough'. However, starting out tough made me better at overcoming obstacles and challenges. I was able to leverage my years of business experience so I was not backing down, instead I 'doubled-down.' I doubled up on advertising and exposure so we had no dead space. For example in the cold, quiet months of winter, we were out at galas and social events, ensuring we were a part of the scene and not hiding away until Spring arrived.

Another valuable lesson I learned was to 'hire well and hire slow'. My team is 'family' and we intentionally created it to be this way, so I want the right people surrounding me. We do a lot together outside of work like bowling nights, regular meetings at local restaurants and boating and bbqs on Summer weekends.

WHAT WORKS

We make good use of social media platforms and with the addition of our social media manager we can take it to the next level. Facebook, Instagram and LinkedIn are our more successful sites that we get clients from.

Once a person realizes they have a business and are not just a real estate agent, then they will have a better direction of how to brand and market themselves. Regardless of how big or small your team is, you are your brand and you need to show the 'world' you mean business.

Part of our brand differentiation is we are always doing something and always moving forward. I see time and time again, new agents buying billboard space and spending a small fortune on getting their 'face' out there. This simply doesn't work. The 'secret sauce' is to get out there and make a difference.

Lead generation for me does not come in the form of buying lists or cold calling, instead I go talk to people and discuss how I can help their business and how we can collaborate on events. Shaking hands and meeting real people is what drives my business.

The number one difference between our brokerage, Keller-Williams, and all others is culture. The level of collaboration across teams and the amount of selfless sharing makes our brokerage second to none! Also, the education and training that Keller-Williams provides is top notch. Team leaders often join representatives in their training, which is unheard of in the industry. KW is both a technology and training company that spans the globe in reach and yet manages to keep things real with a local feel.

A WORD ON COACHING

As I look back over the years, I have drawn strength from a vast amount of personal and professional coaching and education. I continue to this day to learn as much as I can and absorb education like a sponge.

THE most influential book I have ever read and would recommend to anyone in business is "The Millionaire Real Estate Agent" by Gary

Keller. Yes, the same Keller as in Keller-Williams. He single-handedly set the standard for all other real estate books to follow.

Another name that comes to mind is a great friend Glen McQueenie, who is a multiple franchise owner at Keller-Williams. He has a coaching program and authored books that can help most anyone in the real estate business and I consider him an excellent mentor.

Lastly, Jeff Glover is also an amazing coach and trainer at Keller-Williams. His energy is off the charts and he is worth looking up if you want a great coaching program.

FULL SPECTRUM

I started a renovation/construction business on the side just for my clients because I was sick of clients telling me horror stories about putting down deposits for work to be done and never hearing from the contractor again. Now we offer this as a service and people love it!

We think of our business as a full spectrum one, which offers our clients a whole package deal should they require needs above and beyond their home being sold. Home inspections and staging are also built into our full service plan.

One story that touches me deeply is a widowed client who was taken advantage of at every point when she needed renovations and repairs done on her home. She overpaid on her furnace and air conditioning and window replacements. This story was the catalyst for creating my renovation company to treat people fairly.

NO FAST SOLUTIONS

If I were to start my real estate business over again I would:

- Get more help-hire faster.
- Micro-manage less.
- Realize there are no fast solutions in real estate.
- Niche my business and farm a small area.
- Develop a thick skin, early in my career.
- Become something to someone, not everything to everyone.

Some key learnings I received over the years:

- Stop advertising and spending too much money on needless gimmicks.
- Do not buy leads.
- Prioritize your 'A' list and give back to them.
- Host neighborhood open houses with some wine and cheese.
- Door knock in an area we just sold a house in.
- Develop good, strong working relationships with other out of town real estate agents. This increased our business to 7-8 referrals per month.

Our mission of working with local businesses and charities goes hand in hand with working with Parkbench. Although we have been working this type of system for years, we anticipate the website will elevate us on a more professional level. We also expect businesses to come to us asking to be spotlighted which expands our business exponentially.

The most important people in a successful real estate career are our great clients, who become our raving fans! Also family and friends are very important as they have always been there for me-thank you all!

Cris Kambouris

REACH OUT TO CRIS KAMBOURIS

Mobile: 519-995-7600
Email: info@sellwindsor.ca
Website: www.sellwindsor.com

WHAT CLIENTS ARE SAYING ABOUT CRIS

"We went through both ends of the spectrum of purchasing a new place as well as selling our house with Cris, Janine, and the team. Everything was done in a fast, efficient manner. They were very professional, kept us in the loop along the way, answered questions, and asked for our input as well to meet our goals. Great team to work with to get the job done. Exceeded our expectations, would definitely recommend."

~John & Arife M.

"Great friendly service and communication. The team was knowledgeable and honest. Working with Cris and the team alleviated the stress of selling/buying a home. This is my second time working with Cris and I would not hesitate to call him again for future real estate matters."

~Lori S.

"I just want to reach out and give a big thank you to Cris Kambouris and just say what an amazing agent he is. We have known him for a few years and when my siblings and I lost our parents and had so much to deal with Cris

came to our rescue. He helped us beyond what was expected of him. That was the first time he helped me. Then I returned back to Canada from Europe and needed to find a home but unfortunately not in Windsor, where Cris is based.

My sister contacted him and right away he called me, asked me what I needed, my wants and so on. My problem was I planned to move to Montreal – where I had never been before, needless to say, I didn't know anyone and really was a bit apprehensive cold calling a real estate agent not knowing whom I could trust.

Wow I can't believe how fast Cris worked, and of course, I wasn't even a client but that didn't matter to Cris, right away he contacted some people and expressed my situation and my needs and he led me to a fantastic agent.

Within a few weeks, I found the ideal home and made a new friend. I can't express how thankful and amazed I am at Cris's professionalism, commitment and excellent workmanship he has. He truly is an excellent Real Estate Agent. Caring, thoughtful, committed to helping clients to the best he can. He totally sorted everything out for me even during this difficult COVID nightmare, it didn't stop him. Just unbelievable how committed he was in helping me get what I needed. Thank you so much, Cris, I will always be grateful."

~Anna A.

CHAPTER 8

NASA ENGINEER TURNED REALTOR®

"The heart of my business is being of service and providing value at every opportunity. I need my clients to trust me as they are investing in one of the largest investments of their lifetime."

Juan Munoz
Denver, CO

GET TO KNOW JUAN MUNOZ

Juan is someone who brings a smile and positive energy to any situation. His passion is to help others chase their dreams, whether it is personally, in businesses or in fulfilling their dreams of home-ownership.

Juan loves the whole process of real estate and has a genuine interest in hearing people out to figure out their needs to better customize his service to them. He is well-grounded and has a service mentality which you will see by the way he takes care of his clients. His professionalism, responsiveness, attention to detail and listening skills are unparalleled. Real estate isn't about him, it is about you and your needs. This all comes from his heart and daily dedication to continual learning and studying the real estate market. He openly says he is addicted to coffee and real estate and his PASSION shows!

Outside of real estate, Juan was previously a NASA engineer who once spoke to an Astronaut on the cell phone while still in orbit. Juan loves sports, spending time with his family hiking, snowboarding, going on road trips, having dance parties with his daughter, running around with his son and spending time with his lovely wife. You will also find Juan involved in his community and volunteering his time.

NASA ENGINEER TURNED REALTOR®

JUAN MUNOZ

As the first child of three, I was looked upon as a role model for my younger siblings. We came from humble beginnings as my mom was a house cleaner and my dad was a pipefitter. Growing up in a blue collar home didn't stop me from pursuing my dreams and it actually motivated me to pursue a higher education and obtained a bachelor and master degrees. Both my parents taught me the importance of hard work and being a good person above all else.

They immigrated from Mexico and came to America to give me a better life. It was my mom who was the disciplinary of the two, and she always told me to work hard and "hit the books!" I can still hear her words, *"Be better than the next person and it's up to you to make things happen"* which instilled the competitive nature in me. I translated that to mean improve upon myself every day and not to rely on others in order to reach my goals.

As the captain of our basketball team and quarterback of my football team I was always in a leadership position and took my roles seriously. These responsibilities helped me create the foundations of my business.

I used to help my mom clean houses when I was younger. She gave me everything and wanted the best for me. She gave me my first pair of Nike shoes, which back then, was a significant amount of money. At the time, I didn't fully appreciate all the things she gave me but I certainly do now.

These values and morals have spilled into my adult life and as a father I am passing them along to my children. Although I like to spoil my little ones, I also know there is a balance of a better life that should not be taken for granted.

FROM NASA TO FIXING FLIPS

As a human being I am always in search of learning new things and in particular, how to talk to people and find a true connection with them. I am big on taking personal assessments like the Strength Finders test, DISC Profile and Myers-Briggs Personality Test which has me pegged as a positive person who thrives on getting things done and can communicate and connect with people well. I was an engineer at the time, so this was a departure from what a typical engineer would 'look' like and my peers' test results showed that.

I was a financial advisor for a brief period of time during the time I was working at NASA and before I moved to Denver. Flipping houses, wholesaling and rental properties were great investments and I soon learned that getting my real estate license would be very helpful to my bottom line and realized it was my strength of helping people buy and sell homes.

I paid my way through college at Texas A&M University, so I am no stranger to hard work and sacrifice. As the eldest son, I feel like I have the highest responsibility on a financial and role model level, so part of my 'why' is to help my parents in their retirement.

It was a big thing when I got my first house. I moved from Seattle working at Boeing renting an apartment to Houston to working at NASA, International Space Station and buying a house.

I got my license in 2017 in Colorado, and worked it part time. I did better than most agents working the business full time so in 2022 I made the commitment to work it full time and be the team leader and mentor at my brokerage. Don't get me wrong, I was hesitant and a little scared to make the jump into real estate fully but I took the risk regardless with the support from friends and family who knew real estate is my passion.

It was a calculated risk but it was the 'right' time for me based on my belief system and the network of clients I have helped and all the referrals I had been receiving due to my past work that everyone seemed to appreciate. I had an established network and many Google 5 Star reviews so I felt confident to make the leap of faith.

"MAYOR OF MIDTOWN"

When my wife and I were looking for a house we met a listing agent who dismissed us as potential clients due to what I felt was the color of our skin and casual wear. She wouldn't even talk to us because she stereotyped us as being incapable of making the home purchase. Everybody should be treated the same regardless of their ethnicity or diversity. This helped propel me into real estate further as I knew I could do better than that!

Today, I enjoy a great life in my community as I drive around in my golf cart waving 'hi' at my neighbors. As the unofficial *"Mayor of Midtown"* I head up the 'meet and greet welcoming committee.' We make sure that people feel part of our community from the minute they move here by connecting them to people who have similar likes or hobby interests.

As an active member of the social committee here, I get involved in a lot of different community events. One of my favorite ones is helping kids decorate their bikes for the parade on the July 4th holiday. They follow me behind my golf cart to the local park where hot dogs, cake, ice cream and balloons await!

I can't emphasize enough how dog-friendly our city is. You can take your dog almost anywhere you want to go. We have an 18 year-old chihuahua and she is a huge part of our family so we want her to come with us as much as she can.

BEST OF BOTH WORLDS

As a rule of thumb, if you are coming from out of town or state, you can expect to pay about $3500.00 per month(Texas as an example) compared to about $2500.00 per month here in Colorado for the same priced house.

If you love the outdoors, then jumping in your car in any direction will take you to hiking and biking trails, lakes, fishing spots or skiing in the Rocky mountains. Although it is a four-season state, we have 300 days of sunshine to enjoy, so you can get the best of both worlds. Endless breweries, restaurants and coffee shops are there to choose from. Cabins in the mountains are popular but you have to watch out for moose and keep one eye over your shoulder for bears!

The Denver Broncos are the center of attention here and I love attending tailgates and games. The Colorado Avalanche, Colorado Rockies and Denver Nuggets all bring in the crowds.

Denver has a real mix of people with a lot of diversity including young families, singles, an active LBGTQ community and so much more. Yes, there are the older homes with big yards but you can also find a lot of new builds or condo living styles. If you want more information about my hometown, please feel free to contact me.

VALUE, VALUE, VALUE

When I think about what some of the key factors are that led me to my success I have a list!

- I have always learned and will continue to learn and master my craft.
- I have a genuine connection with people.
- When people talk, I listen.
- I provide value to everyone I can. Yes, I will help you shovel your driveway.
- I leverage my contacts and connections to help my clients and neighbors.

- I am hard-working and will go above and beyond and have a good work ethic.
- I have integrity and I am ethical.

Regardless of what you do in life, there will be ups and downs and people shutting doors and saying 'no' to your face. This happens to me but I choose to take the lessons and learn from them to improve everyday. It's also important to celebrate the small wins along the way as this will keep you motivated to continue towards your goals.

The heart of my business is being of service and providing value at every opportunity. I need my clients to trust me as they are investing in one of the largest investments of their lifetime. Showing social proof is equally important as people will seek you out on the internet before they pick up their phone.

'Get out of your own way' is key as it allows you the freedom to give yourself permission to go all in! *"I can do it"* needs to become your daily mantra until you can actually 'feel' it happening. No one is going to hold you accountable but yourself and being humble is necessary in order for you to grow.

My investment in coaching and training has cost me tens of thousands of dollars but it was worth every penny! Investing in yourself will help you learn what works for you and more importantly, what doesn't. You get out of it what you put into it-simple.

CREATING GENERATIONAL WEALTH AND AGENT EXPANSION

A big goal of mine is to make it big. I want an office with a team and a business that is solid enough to transition to my children one day- if they choose to, of course. I want to be in the position to run the business to support and encourage my agents to reach their full potential.

I am currently expanding my business and I am looking for agents who share the same values as I do. I want to create a 'work family' who supports each other, who has a positive mindset, and who helps each other through tough times.

I have automated systems in place to help create lead generation. I can provide training, scripts and CRM programs to help with our database. Mindset training will also be on top of the list to help my team grow on both a personal and professional level. My social media presence is high and I am very good at negotiation tactics. I am looking to expand by hiring a full time assistant who is local to the area.

BASED ON EXPERIENCE

I have learned what works best for me and my business but I can drill it down to a few pointers.

Don't...

- Talk about clients
- Air dirty laundry.
- Show frustrations outwards- keep it cool.
- Boast about the deals you make.
- Overload yourself. The pressure creates anxiety.
- Be a secret agent

Do...

- Time block.(personal time as well)
- Stick to schedule/calendar.
- Talk to lenders, brokers- keep communication flowing.
- Keep on top of trends.
- Become THE go-to person.
- Have good relationships with other agents.
- Give other agents reviews.
- Be professional and respectful.

Become a good learner and choose books or podcasts that fuel your passion. I personally recommend the book, *"Atomic Habits"* by James Clear. Creating habits is really important to getting stuff done! Habits like time blocking or posting X number of times a week on your social media platforms. Whatever it is, just keep doing it. *"The Millionaire*

Agent" by Gary Keller is another favorite of mine. Although this book is dated, the information inside is timeless. Pick it up, it's worth it.

Supporting local businesses is a great thing to do. Working with Parkbench is leveraging my ability to get in front of more people to help fellow small business owners. I can relate to many of these people as we are all entrepreneurs working towards making our lives better.

I like to look for a win-win-win with every interaction I come across. Providing small business owners the opportunity to be interviewed and marketed through the Parkbench website and my social media outlets is a win for all of us.

GRATITUDE

First and foremost I want to thank my parents for the sacrifices they made to get into America to give us a better way of life. I have an education that I may not have had if we stayed in Mexico. They instilled in me a higher work ethic and determination which has got me to where I am today.

My wife, Jacqueline and my kids, Michael Juan and Mialana, I want to thank you for being my 'Why' and keeping it as strong as it is. I can't forget our little dog Chiquita, who keeps the spirit alive!

I've had many coaches, mentors, family members and friends who never gave up on me and helped me develop along the way.

If life presents you with an opportunity and you have a passion for it-go for it! Don't have regrets and don't look back!

Juan Munoz

REACH OUT TO JUAN MUNOZ

juan@homesindenvernow.com
www.homesindenvernow.com
http://instagram.com/juanmunozrealestate
https://www.facebook.com/juanmunozrealtor/
https://www.linkedin.com/in/munoz-juan

WHAT CLIENTS ARE SAYING ABOUT JUAN

"We cannot say enough good things about Juan. He literally went the extra 20 miles for us the entire home selling process. He truly was a full service realtor and went above and beyond to make it as minimally intrusive in our lives and get us the highest profits we didn't even think were possible. I would recommend Juan to anyone looking for a home – in any financial situation – with any preferences – because he will work hard to help you find your dream home and advise you throughout the process as if you were family. If you are looking to buy or sell, choose Juan – and let his hard work ethic, loyalty, and ingenuity work for you and your home sale."

~ Allison T.

"When I say that Juan was a Godsend for our family, this is not an exaggeration. Our family was looking for a new home for nearly 6 months and continued to lose homes (primarily in Midtown), despite making aggressive offers. We knew that Juan was a reputable realtor and a well-connected, Midtown expert. So we reached out to Juan hoping that he might know of

some more homes coming up that met our needs. Juan very quickly connected us with multiple sellers, and we ultimately went under contract on one of them. We could not be more happy with our home (our favorite of any we had seen in Midtown) or more thankful to have had Juan's help. If you want to buy or sell, Juan is who you should contact!"

~ Steph T.

"We really enjoyed working with Juan. He's very dedicated to his clients and works hard to make the selling process as simple as possible. Our home sold quickly at our asking price, we were thrilled! Definitely recommend"

~ Kali O.

CHAPTER 9

JUMPING OFF A CLIFF WITHOUT A PARACHUTE

" Relationships are formed at every level of contact. Many of my clients say, "Sherri is not my Realtor®; she's family." These people are near to my heart, but they also send me bountiful referrals of which I am eternally grateful."

Sherri Murphy
Southlake, TX

GET TO KNOW SHERRI MURPHY

I am a Native Texan and grew up here in the DFW area. I have been a licensed agent for over 20 years, and I am also a Certified Military Relocation Specialist and Luxury Home Specialist with the National Association of Realtors. I am a partner with Homes for Heroes which allows me to give back to our first responders, teachers, medical staff, and military to thank them for their service and contribution to our country and communities.

I absolutely love my clients and my goal is to exceed all expectations in the buying and selling process. Every client's needs are different, and I work to gain insight into my client's desires and goals through my Consultations. This allows me to find the right home, at the right price for my buyer, while not missing anything in the market. I enjoy assisting my sellers in selling their home with ease and getting the best price possible in the time frame they have to sell within.

My background in real estate is vast and includes Residential & REO Sales, Property Management and Mortgage Lending, which allows me to give my clients a positive and stress-free experience while building relationships that last a lifetime. Working with me will be an experience you will not soon forget, and I will be your Trusted Real Estate Advisor and friend for life!

JUMPING OFF A CLIFF WITHOUT A PARACHUTE

SHERRI MURPHY

I grew up in the Dallas/Fort Worth area near Southlake Texas, which at the time was barely a blip on the map. It was often overshadowed by Fort Worth to the Southwest and Dallas to the Southeast. It has since grown and expanded into a highly sought-after area rich in both cultural and natural beauty. Although my journey took me away to Houston and then New Jersey for a short time, I returned to my roots in Texas and call Southlake 'home'.

ABOUT THIS LITTLE TOWN CALLED SOUTHLAKE

I remember the days when it was only a two-lane road with one traffic light signal in the middle of town and felt like we were in the middle of nowhere. Long gone are those days as our little town has blossomed into a thriving, bustling and affluent community of over 32,000 people. For various reasons and the Covid Pandemic is no exception, people from across the country are wanting to live here and raise their families in Southlake because our schools are rated amongst the best in the State. In addition, the location is ideal, being minutes from DFW International Airport and centrally located between Dallas and Fort

Worth. Southlake also has amazing restaurants, shopping, and entertainment.

A vivid story comes to mind that best describes the rapid expansion of Southlake over the years. I was asked by a lovely senior couple to help them sell their house as they wanted to retire elsewhere. After they got out of college they married and purchased a quaint 3-bedroom ranch style house on 4.8 acres of land complete with a barn and turnout for their horse and goats. They paid $99,000 27 years ago and we recently sold it for a whopping $1.475 million! They were ecstatic as they turned around and paid cash for their dream home on a peaceful lake front property large enough to accommodate their four-legged 'family members' — complete with a boat dock and swimming pool!

SCRAPING STICKERS OFF WINDOWS

Since I was a child, I was always fascinated with real estate. Both my grandfather and uncle were homebuilders and developers and often reached out to my parents to offer them some extra work on the side. My parents had a hard time making ends meet so this work was welcomed. As the 'clean-up crew' we would go in at various stages of construction and clean for the crews and do the final clean before it went to market. One of my jobs was scraping stickers off windows and ensuring they were sparkling clean.

This experience left me with ambitions to be an architect, builder, and interior designer. However, my parents had other things in mind for me. *"You need to be a secretary. Those jobs are not secure and not made for a woman"*. These words were not what I wanted to hear but to make them happy and proud of me, I obliged. So off I went to college, working and paying my own way through. Guess what? I got bored very quickly.

I decided to apply as a payment processor at Finance America, a company specializing in home improvement loans for homeowners. I soon moved up the ladder and became the youngest branch manager in the history of the company. I was only 22 years old and managing a branch in Houston! Then the oil bust of the 1980s hit, and it hit hard.

Everything came to a grinding halt. Foreclosures were stacking up and people literally mailed in their keys to their financial institutions and walked away from their homes and defaulted mortgages.

Lucky for me, Verex Assurance hired me as an asset manager to help with these foreclosures. But to list a property for sale and negotiate the contracts, I had to have my real estate license, so I did just that. I was very successful and helped a lot of people get out of foreclosure. Houston, in particular, was one of the hardest hit by this recession and communities were like ghost towns — people just up and left.

This led me to volunteer for the Houston Neighborhood Revitalization Program. I would speak at Neighborhood HOAs (Homeowners Associations), and I loved educating the homeowners about the repercussions of foreclosure and helping people save their homes.

At this point in my career, I was hired into the RTC (Resolution Trust Corporation) which took me to New Jersey. This was a five-year program aimed at helping failing savings and loans. We would package the mortgages and foreclosed properties, including commercial properties, and sell them on Wall Street. Kislak Real Estate and Property Management was a company that bought large segments of the commercial foreclosures and brought these properties up to a level of income-producing assets which were then sold back on the open market. They sought me out and offered me a position as a Property Manager over some of these portfolios in the States of New Jersey, Pennsylvania, and New York. Of course, I had to have my real estate license in order to do property management — so I did!

WITH JUST MY CLOTHES AND MAKEUP

My career had taken shape and set me up to be a successful real estate agent. But as in my career, my personal life also took a few twists and turns. After spending over six years in New Jersey, I was tired of shoveling snow and homesick for Texas, so we moved back to the Dallas/Fort Worth area. Back in Texas, I spent seven years as a Mortgage Loan Officer and two years as a Marketing Director for a Mortgage Company before going back to where my passion really was, in the real estate industry.

And then, after 20 years of marriage, I found myself in a difficult divorce. I left the house with an armful of clothes, my makeup and car keys. I started rebuilding my life and was offered a job as the Market Center Administrator at a Keller Williams real estate office about an hour away. Roughly a year later, my mother fell ill and became handicapped. I found myself needing to move closer to her to help out. When I put the word out that I was looking for a job closer to home, a small, but well-known real estate team in the area hired me on the spot as their listing and transaction coordinator.

It was there that I completely blossomed, and things fell into place. The leaders approached me one day out of the clear blue and said, *"You really need to be in sales."* I had just put all my savings into buying a house a few doors down from my mom, and I had nothing to fall back on. I told them I needed time to think and pray about it. God was persistent in His message! The signs around me could not be ignored. I went back a week later and told my leaders, *"I am jumping off a cliff without a parachute or a net to catch me. But I am doing this!"* Failure was not an option, and in my case, it was my motivator!

Within 30 days I had my first transaction and it just steamrolled from there. My goal was to close $5 million of sales in my first year (which technically was only 10 months since I accepted the new job at the end of February), but I did $12 million!! My passion took over and I hopped out of bed every day with a big smile on my face. "Who am I going to meet and sell a home to today?" was my driving force.

BUILDING RELATIONSHIPS THROUGH PHILANTHROPIC WORK

A key factor to my success as an agent, but more so as a person, is the lifelong relationships I have formed through the volunteer work I do within my community. It makes me feel good to help others in need. It started in the 80s with the Neighborhood Revitalization Program. Then when my children were in school, I was heavily involved in my kids' band fundraisers. I was also involved in The National Charity League, a mother/daughter organization that does philanthropy work for various causes. The premise is that mothers and daughters work together from 8th grade to high school graduation with various philanthropies, to help educate our daughters and prepare them for college and the world, as adults. Not only do you do volunteer work, but the mothers and even the daughters have monthly meetings. The League has a board of directors that serve terms with various responsibilities.

My desire to help people continued to be strong after my children graduated and left home, so when my son joined the Airforce, I focused my philanthropic efforts on helping veterans. But I wasn't stopping there. With the help of my broker, I created a successful blood drive to help replenish the blood banks that were in desperate need of blood during and after COVID. People were lining up to donate and help! In addition, in January of this year, I gathered my team together for a Food Drive to help replenish food banks after the holidays. Again, a very important way to give back to people in need.

I also partner with Homes for Heroes, a non-profit organization that sprung from the ashes of 911. I give generously with a portion of my commission going to help support the Heroes in our community, so that they receive a portion of their closing costs back through Homes for Heroes.

WHAT GOES AROUND, COMES AROUND

Relationships are formed at every level of contact. Many of my clients say, *"Sherri is not my Realtor®; she's family."* These people are near to my heart, but they also send me bountiful referrals of which I am eternally grateful.

With the help from Parkbench and my new website, I am meeting more new people and directing them to various businesses and local events to help welcome them to our community. I really love promoting people and their businesses through my interviews and online platforms.

I have solidified my role as a Local Leader® in my community. People trust me and rely on me as a connector, and I am often approached to refer them to a good plumber or a good place to take their family for pizza. Whatever the case may be, I am a human rolodex and I love it!

THE GOLDEN RULES OF SUCCESS

Listen, listen, listen. The number one rule, in my books, is to listen to people with every chance I can. We are so busy in life, and we miss so much about a person unless we truly take the time to put everything on pause and just "listen" to what someone has to say. Have you just taken the time to ask someone "How do you feel today?" You can find out so much about a person if you do. And when the conversation is done, that may have been the best thing that happened to them all day. Just a person to lend an ear and listen to them. Just like a smile, you never know when you will help someone by just listening.

My mother instilled in me, *"Do unto others as they would do unto you."* The Golden Rule is at the heart of my existence and has served me well over the years. It's God's way. This can be extended far beyond the person sitting in front of you. For instance, if I see someone has lost their pet and posts it on Facebook, I will reach out to them and send a card to cheer them up or a card of congratulations on a job promotion, etc. Whatever the case may be, I like to send a card to let them know I am thinking of them. I hand-write up to 10 notes every day and mail them to clients, friends, family, anyone I may come in contact with. I don't include a business card as I believe this cheapens the intent behind the note. The intent is to say "Hi, I care about you." That's it. No hidden agendas.

Consistency. Consistency. Consistency. Several years ago, I implemented a morning routine that propelled me forward in life. Today I still have the same routine. I grab a hot cup of coffee, sit down at my desk, and read a few pages in the Bible every day. Then I write my gratitude, and affirmations. I even keep a vision board next to my desk with my active goals and aspirations. It helps me to keep my vision clear and sets my attitude for the day. Finally, while I am getting ready for work, I listen to something motivational. Either a sermon from one of my favorite Pastors, or a motivational recording on YouTube, etc. I believe in the Law of Attraction; positivity attracts the positive! This along with consistency and a routine are habits that are entrenched in my existence and are the cornerstone of every successful person out there.

CARING CONNECTIONS

Making the time to reach out by phone or face-to-face is also important for my relationships with people. Social media is a great way to keep up with what's going on in people's lives. For instance, I called a high school friend that I reconnected with when I found out her son was in a horrible accident and was now at the mercy of a wheelchair. This hit me hard as I realized that life can change so fast, in the blink of an eye. It was important that I talked to her as so many people want to hide behind online posts versus making a direct connection.

During the Covid pandemic I called people and simply asked them, "Do you need anything?" I was willing to get them food or help in any way possible. I ended up ordering 'Encouragement Cards' and mailed them out to people I knew. "You do not know how much I needed that" was a common response I received. One never knows when you can touch somebody, and it fills my heart when I know I have.

I love 'pop-byes' because I can be spontaneous, and people really get a kick out of them. In the spring, for instance, I left gardening gloves, a shovel, and seeds, etc. for people to use. The next thing I knew, a client posted on social media, "just in time for gardening today!", and posted a picture of the gloves and shovel, now dirty form the soil, and she tagged me in the post and thanked me. This wasn't the first time it had happened. Often, people post a photo of the items I pop by with on Facebook and give me a shout out.

I WILL FIND A WAY

A big reason for my success is I always try to find solutions. I am stubborn and I don't give up easily! I will find a way to get an offer accepted. For example, I had a client moving from California and we were having a difficult time getting a home since the market was crazy, and most listings were being sold well over listed price with multiple offers.

We found a house that they fell in love with but knew we would be up against a bidding war. Nonetheless, they wanted to proceed so I got creative with the offer. Instead of the usual 1% earnest money we offered 3%, and we gave them a three-day option period versus five days and $500 a day versus a lower amount that most offer, i.e., $100 a day. We needed to wow the seller with the offer, so we went one step further and offered $56,000 over the asking price. I also asked the selling agent what was important to them and found out they needed a lease back for three weeks. We offered them a free lease back so they could stay in their home while they waited on their move.

Up against 18 other offers, ours was the most outstanding so it was accepted and within hours we had an executed contract in our inbox! Communication is key and a simple "What's important to your seller" can go a long way.

Communicating with the buyer (or your seller) throughout the transaction is also vital. Even more important, keeping in contact with them after the sale closes. Don't let it be just another transaction. Let your client know how grateful you are for their trust in you as their real estate advisor.

BUILDING MY TEAM

I currently have two new agents working with me and I am excited for our future together. I choose my teammates based largely on who they are and why they want to work in this industry. The two people I have chosen couldn't be more different from each other except they both have huge hearts and are passionate about being 'all in!'

A willingness to learn and being part of something larger than themselves are two components that are non-negotiable to be part of my venture. My goal is to have six agents by 2023 with an assistant to help with the daily operations.

My bigger vision is to have a staging company, storage units, moving truck(s) and an Airbnb to help transitioning clients. All of this would support my core business, increase my revenue, and meet our clients' needs. I am also writing a series of books about the home buying process, the selling process, and home maintenance that I will provide to my clients when I meet with them.

ADVICE TO MY YOUNGER SELF

A simple list of a few things I would do and not do if I started over again:

I wish I had…

- Followed my heart initially out of high school and pursued my passion.
- Never second guessed myself in certain situations and trusted my gut instinct.
- Researched companies better by checking reviews and asking questions before I invested in their technology/lead generation.
- Started time-blocking earlier in life — *especially my personal time.*
- Finished College — I was so close!

I wish I hadn't…

- Cold called without a solid plan laid out for follow up or farming.
- Paid for lead generation. (The future buyer or seller is embedded in the last transaction.)
- Wasted time. Time can be our enemy and I should have stewarded it and tended to it better.

All this being said, it's important to keep the momentum going. Do one thing that propels your business forward every day. Consistency breeds success.

I LOVE BOOKS AND LEARNING

Reading and continuing to learn is one of the most important activities that anyone can do. When I started my career, I read books like, *Who Moved My Cheese*, *Go for No!*, and *The One Minute Manager*. Now, books by John Maxwell, who is an amazing thought leader in leadership and management line my bookshelves. He is likely one of my favorite authors and coaches. *No Limits- Blow the Cap Off Your Capacity* is my all-time favorite. The basic premise is that people create false ceilings for themselves and can't get past those limitations. So don't put a lid on what you think you can do!

I DON'T WORK A DAY IN MY LIFE

We've all heard these words spilling out of Facebook and Instagram posts but what does it really mean? For me, it means I am grateful to be doing what I love, with people I love, and for reasons I am blessed to have. Being a real estate agent isn't a job for me — it's a lifestyle, a choice, and my passion for which I am eternally grateful.

Sherri Murphy

REACH OUT TO SHERRI MURPHY

SHERRI MURPHY, REALTOR® and Team Lead
Coldwell Banker Realty
850 E. State Highway 114, Ste. 100
Southlake, TX 76092
C. 817.929.2059 | License #: 0704592
Sherri@TheUltimateREGroup.com

WHAT CLIENTS ARE SAYING ABOUT SHERRI

"Sherri is quite literally the best Realtor® we have ever had the honor to work with. She is more than a Realtor®, she is a friend! She truly cares about you from day 1 and continues to be a guide to this day! We consider Sherri part of our family forever. She works around the clock and that is no joke. Her thoughtfulness and personal attention are second to none! We love Sherri! We bought and sold with Sherri twice now in Southlake and Colleyville. She is our Realtor® for life!"

~Kristen B.

"Sherri was extremely professional, helpful, knowledgeable, and patient as we decided to make a change after 32 years. She took our calls, texts, emails at every hour and was swift and kind in her response. I can't imagine selling our property of 32 years and buying another without Sherri. She helped us navigate a world we hadn't been a part of in decades with the utmost compassion

and understanding. We have made a new forever friend in Sherri and we are so very thankful she was on this journey with us."

~Lezah

"Sherri was amazing as we needed to sell our mom's home after she passed away. From the beginning Sherri was always professional and offered realistic recommendations as we did not want to spend a great deal "preparing" for the sale. Throughout the process she kept my sisters and I updated as to what was happening and what the next steps were. She always answered any of the questions that we asked throughout the process. I would definitely recommend her as you are looking for a real estate agent."

~Deanna H.

CHAPTER 10

WHAT IS THE WORST THAT CAN HAPPEN?

" A great salesperson will exhaust all avenues before giving up. I have learned my craft from the best in the business and yes I am proud to say that the word 'NO' is not in my vocabulary."

Suzanne Anderson
Fort McMurray, AB

GET TO KNOW SUZANNE ANDERSON

I'm an international, award-winning REALTOR® with RE/MAX® Fort McMurray since 2001, and owner/team leader of the Anderson Sharks Team. My real estate license covers commercial, residential, rural, and property management, so no matter what your real estate needs, we have the expertise and knowledge to help buy or sell your home or business.

WHAT IS THE WORST THAT CAN HAPPEN?

SUZANNE ANDERSON

THIS IS HOW I WORK

I loosely joke that I am available 24-7, and my clients appreciate my high level of accessibility but if you try calling me at 3:00am, you will likely get my voicemail. It's a bit of a misnomer that real estate agents are truly available all the time, but let's face it, we all have lives outside of our business. The truth is, as agents, we are managing expectations for a whole team of people so it stands to reason that we are a quick call away at any time.

I have found that if you, as an agent, are honest and upfront with your clients then it will be a much more pleasant experience for them and yourself as well. I think people refer others to me primarily because I am a tough negotiator and I get the job done. I love what I do, and I am truly honoured to have so many amazing clients to work with!

A "3-SHIFT TOWN"

Fort McMurray, Alberta, or 'Fort Mac' as we locals like to call it, has been my home since 1998. I grew up in Halifax, NS, moved to Toronto,

ON for a brief stint, then I was off to Fort Mac. When I landed in the town my first words were, *"Who would want to live here?"* What I thought was going to be a short period of time ended up being 24 years and I have no intention of ever leaving.

This town has been met with unprecedented 'bad luck' for several years, but I am glad to say it's on the upswing once again. The 2016 Horse River wildfire left our town burnt to the ground. It would have been easy for me to pull up my stakes and find another place to live, but I was determined to help rebuild my home and community.

Well known for its oil and gas industry, it has been coined the 'three shift town' as life revolves around the shift work at the oil rigs and oilsands. Many people have historically moved here because of job offers but stay because they ultimately build their lives here. One of the most affordable places to live in Canada, Fort McMurray is attractive to many 'remote' workers who want a quiet, peaceful lifestyle.

Any nature enthusiast will find epic adventures just a step from their front door. From dog sledding to fishing to enjoying the Northern Lights, this Alberta town has a lot to offer. If business investment is your thing, then you may want to consider the "Alberta Advantage." Having the lowest corporate tax rate in Canada at 8% and uber municipal incentives like a five-year tax exemption in our downtown district, this region is poised for success!

HIDING MY COOKIES

Like most of the residents, I too moved here for a job. Imagine getting off the plane and being hit with -37°C winter weather! That was just the beginning. I couldn't start my rental car and so I had to use my hairdryer on the block heater to get the motor running. Prompting me to once again ask myself, "Who would want to live here?"

One night I decided to visit the local watering hole, Bailey's Pub, and struck up a conversation with the bartender. I soon learned he was the local RE/MAX® agent. At the time, I was living out of a suitcase and was growing tired of the non-stop travel, but even so, I wasn't looking for a change in career. I knew I wanted to put down some roots but never entertained the idea of real estate nor living in Fort Mac long-term for that matter.

After being introduced to some of his friends and clients that night I felt a real sense of community. He told me I should be a real estate agent and I'd fit right in. Soon after, my job became obsolete, and I was faced with a decision to make. *"What's the worst that can happen?"* I thought to myself, so I took his advice, and the rest is history.

It didn't take long before I chose a broker, as there were only four to choose from at the time. When I stepped into the RE/MAX® office, I knew this was my forever home. The office was vibrating with enthusiasm and the broker was so dynamic I knew this is where I wanted to be. Furthermore, Gail Malloy, who was the office manager (aka 'mother-hen') was so accommodating and supportive of all us agents. She was a breath of fresh air.

Although the office encouraged collaboration, I learned I had to 'hide my cookies' — at least some of them. Regardless, there will be those people who want to take advantage of you when you start out, so don't lay all your cards on the table.

POSTER CHILD

Fort McMurray is all too often spoken of as an oil and gas town. I believe this isn't justified given the diversity of economics and cultural impact that this small, but powerful little town has to offer.

Being a real estate agent allows me to be connected to my community unlike any other profession. I am now often referred to as the "Posterchild of Fort Mac" by my clients and I love it!!

The Métis Nation will be opening their Bison/Buffalo Park and I was helpful in securing the land for this development. I was invited to their ceremony this year and was filled with the spirit that they are so well known for.

Being involved in your community is a choice and it is a choice that I embrace. If you choose to be transactional and not part of the connection, then you will struggle. Having deep set relationships is fundamental to a sustainable and successful real estate business.

NO IS NOT IN MY VOCABULARY

When I worked as I sales trainer, before getting into real estate, I was asked, "How do you go from being a good sales agent to a great sales agent?" The difference between a good sales person and a great salesperson, is when you are told NO over and over and you start to think there is no hope in getting the deal done. A good sales person will say to their client, "I tried, lets move on," but a great sales person will ask more questions, deal with the objections, and get the deal done. A great salesperson will exhaust all avenues before giving up. I have learned my craft from the best in the business and yes I am proud to say that the word 'NO' is not in my vocabulary.

ROLL OUT THE RED CARPET

Being a real estate agent is not easy. We make it look easy because we have overcome the challenges, we've been there before, we've made our share of mistakes, and we know what is required. I have built my business on processes, and I rely on them to help my clients gain a better experience.

When I first started out, my business wasn't as structured as it is today. My business background taught me I needed systems and processes to function at a high level. Because I was so new, I was busy creating all these processes myself, but little did I know all I had to do was ask my broker for these. So, I was reinventing the wheel needlessly. Today, my business is on autopilot so I can do a high volume in a short period of time.

I like to roll out the red carpet and show my clients exactly what to expect and how the process will work. One needs to be proactive in this business as your clients depend heavily on your judgment and expertise.

With respect to buyers in particular, the biggest problem amongst agents is they have no follow through. If you want to have a solid business, you need to be accountable not only to your clients but to yourself. Once you have the respect of your clients, they will be committed to you — even without a contract.

To illustrate this, I once had a listing that went stale. Most sellers in this situation are ready to bail and list with someone else. My client did get calls from other agents looking to 'do better' for him, however, my client chose to stick it out the finish line with me. Why? I remained his agent because I had already built a good relationship with him, and he felt loyal to me.

CLOSE TO MY HEART

I involve myself in local charities and clubs that are close to my heart. For example, our local Children's Miracle Network chapter receives donations from myself and other agents in the RE/MAX® office. I lost my brother from cancer so working for this cause resonates with me at a very personal level.

RE/MAX® Worldwide plays a significant role in raising millions and millions of dollars around the world each year by each agent pledging a minimum of $25.00 from each sale towards the Children's Miracle Network.

At a local level, I volunteered tirelessly as both a soccer and hockey mom as my daughter was very active in sports. I also involve myself in raising funds for other charities within my community, particularly for Fort McMurray's homeless population.

THE ANDERSON SHARKS

Up until recently I had a small team of three agents, but unfortunately one member passed away and the other retired. I have had a few people approach me to be on my team and I am in the process of deciding on who will be a good fit. So, if you want to become a 'Shark' come see me!

If you want to learn how to drive, attend driving school. The same holds true for real estate. If you want to succeed in real estate, then attend classes, coaching, and/or read a lot of books. I was involved in the Richard Robin's coaching program for six years which was instrumental to my success.

I also was mentored by the real estate lawyer who I sent business to. He too had his real estate license and would walk me through the various requirements of the contracts and other related business dealings. I am forever grateful to him.

Sometimes our business can be cutthroat as there are white sharks everywhere! In our small town, people like this don't tend to stick around but they can exist. I'm a shark because I get things done as opposed to the shark that bites for the sake of biting! I'm more like a *'Bruce'* — the shark from the movie *Finding Nemo* who is friendly but tough enough to get the sale and make it happen.

THE QUEEN OF THE TRAILER PARKS

One of the best pieces of advice I can give, based on my experience, is to do what others are not willing to do and then be the best at it. This is exactly what I did in the beginning of my career. I went around my office and asked a few of the veteran agents what they don't like to do, and the number one answer was sell trailers. They didn't like it because there wasn't much money in it, and they were difficult to manage but all I saw was cha-ching dollar signs in front of me.

So off I went to door knock and make myself available to these folks. It wasn't long after that I earned my first listing, then another, and another, and so on. Guess what happened next? I became the second highest listing agent in my office! The secret sauce was I learned as much about mobile homes as I could. I became a sponge for information and even went to the manufacturers to find out how they were built.

This was topped off when one of my client's sent me a package with a card attached: "To the Queen of the Trailer Park, thanks for selling mine." This catapulted my business to the point where I decided to become a buyer's agent so I could learn more about that side of the business.

DIAMONDS ARE A GIRL'S BEST FRIEND

I didn't approach my real estate career with anything more than to earn a decent living, however, I have been honored to receive several awards over the years including The Diamond Club, Chairman's Club, the Lifetime Achievement Award and Circle of Legends Club. Obtaining a ranking of the top 1% of RE/MAX worldwide of elite agents in RE/MAX® Sales Organization is truly humbling. Although I win these awards, my true goal is to win for my clients.

I attribute some of my success to lessons I learned along the way. For instance, when I took the Zig Ziglar course I learned to be persistent and never, ever give up! I also learned to get out of my own way by figuring out who I was first to learn how to figure out other people. Learning how people tick is essential for creating a sustainable referral-based business.

BUILDING MY FOUNDATION

My plans are to grow a small team of baby sharks who have go-getter and self-starter attributes. I prefer experienced people to join me as I can add value to them without having to hand-hold throughout the process.

I want to get into real estate coaching soon. While there are numerous business coaches out there, I can offer a hands-on approach as I will continue to help clients with their housing needs. This will offer residual income for me in addition to the money earned through selling.

My dad always had my back and would often encourage me with positive words. "If you believe it, you can achieve it," he would say repetitively. He was always there for me even when I had some crazy stories to tell him. He never discouraged me from doing anything. He alone helped set the foundation for my success. Thank you, Dad!

I also want to thank all my professional associates, teammates, brokers, and clients who have helped shape my business throughout the years. It has been quite a journey and sometimes I feel it is just getting started!

Suzanne Anderson

REACH OUT TO SUZANNE ANDERSON

Suzanne Anderson, MBA, GMA, ABR
Licensed Associate in the Province of Alberta
Anderson Sharks Team
RE/MAX Fort McMurray
website: www.fortmcmurrayhome.com
email: info@suzanneanderson.com
Direct Phone: 1-780-713-9178

WHAT CLIENTS ARE SAYING ABOUT SUZANNE

"We have bought and sold 16 plus homes in many places and have had many realtors to handle our transactions. I can honestly say we have never had a realtor who went above and beyond like Suzanne did for us! She is experienced, and highly knowledgeable in her area of expertise, she is professional in her dealings, and fair and square. A quality that I feel is rare these days. She is real and upfront, with no beating around the bush. If I had to buy in the area again I would seek her out to find me the perfect home. She has my vote, and anyone who hires her to represent them in a sale or purchase will most definitely not be disappointed! I would give her 10 stars if I could."

~ Cindy

"Suzanne, I can't tell you how surreal it is to hold the keys in my hand and look at your letter and read the word suggesting that these are the keys to my home! Thank you so much for helping me along this big, big journey. Thank

you for helping make it possible and helping me with all the details and negotiations. I could not have accomplished it without you Suzanne. I am looking for the change in culture from the west coast here and I'm looking forward to Albertans and the beautiful Alberta landscape. If you are in town sometime, stop by and say hello."

~Alli H.

"Suzanne was very helpful and knowledgeable, answered all our questions and was ready to help at all times.. so grateful to her, our dream of buying our first home came true all thanks to Suzanne."

~Oluchi O.

CHAPTER 11

CONNECTING YOU TO THE COUNTY

" CONNECTIONS ARE AN ESSENTIAL PART OF LIFE. FROM THE MOMENT WE ARE BORN THE CONNECTIONS WE MAKE AND THE BONDS WE DEVELOP ARE ESSENTIAL TO OUR WELLBEING AND OUR HAPPINESS, IF NOT OUR VERY EXISTENCE."

SUZANNE WHITE
PRINCE EDWARD COUNTY, ON

GET TO KNOW SUZANNE WHITE

Suzanne White has been a real estate agent since 2015. She is a people person and has always had a strong interest in houses and design. As a child she and her mother would often go to Open Houses or look at model homes - not that they were intending to move, but her mom enjoyed getting decorating ideas and Suzanne loved the architecture and layouts.

In addition to assisting people with buying and selling properties she was a high school teacher for over 30 years working with students in a variety of subject areas as well as being a guidance counselor. She did both careers for 6 years and then left teaching to become a full time real estate agent. Teaching was an excellent background for real estate as it taught her a lot about dealing with a large variety of personalities and also gave her great community connections.

As a lifelong learner, Suzanne is continually educating herself about the local market and keeping up to date with best practices for real estate transactions. She also encourages her clients to be fully educated themselves and spends a lot of time ensuring they fully understand the process and sending them lots of listings and information so they feel extremely comfortable with their decisions.

CONNECTING YOU TO THE COUNTY

SUZANNE WHITE

Connections are an essential part of life. From the moment we are born the connections we make and the bonds we develop are essential to our wellbeing and our happiness, if not our very existence.

Transitions are unavoidable. We move from childhood, through the teenage years, to adulthood. We change careers, friends, life partners, residences. Some transitions are purposeful, fun, and exciting while others are fraught with anxiety, disappointment, anger, or a sense of loss. Regardless of the type of transition, connections can make the process smoother and much more enjoyable.

When my husband and I moved from Whitby to Prince Edward County in 2000, we were purposefully leaving an increasingly expanding city with more traffic, more noise, more pollution, and choosing a location with small communities, lots of farmland and, being an island, surrounded by water.

My husband is a windsurfer and I love to garden so the move held anticipated pleasures for us both. But we were also leaving behind strong friendships forged from childhood, and family. We were moving to a place where we knew no one and had zero connections.

We, thankfully, moved somewhere that is incredibly community-minded and where the idea of being a good neighbour is a badge of honour. This is a place where if your car breaks down on the road someone will stop to assist you within minutes. Where people wave as they pass one another. Where the person at the bank or in the check-out lane at the grocery store knows your name and will stop for a chat.

My co-workers in Whitby joked that we were "moving back to the Seventies." This seemed to be true based on the music they were playing on the local radio stations once we arrived, but to be honest, it was more like the 50s in some respects. In the first week in our new home, our next-door neighbour came over to introduce herself — and brought us a coffee cake! It was the sweetest thing. I felt like I was in an episode of *Leave it to Beaver*.

Prince Edward County is a world unto itself. It was, in part, formed by United Empire Loyalists, fleeing from war in the United States. Many families here can trace their roots back to those origins. There are some locals who suggest that unless you are at least six to seven generations "County" you aren't really from the area. At the point of our move, I was a teacher. Being in education allowed me to get connected with many of those long-time family names that can be seen on stores and roads and so many mailboxes. I got to know the different branches of the families as I heard "Oh, I'm not related to those Prinzens or Vaders or Leavitts . . ." But they would still stick up for one another like brothers if anyone made a disparaging remark about one of their second cousins three times removed on their mother's side. And I will add that the students at the local high school are some of the kindest, most generous teenagers I have ever worked with. I have a deep love and appreciation for youth in general, but the ones here hold a special place in my heart.

My husband and I were both teachers, at the time. I taught at the local high school for 21 years, teaching everything from social sciences to co-op, English, special education, and guidance. It was a wonderful experience, and it gave me the opportunity to meet thousands of wonderful people.

There are good and bad things about teaching in a small community. I once had a student ask me if we had had a party on the weekend. I said no and asked why he thought that. His response was that when he passed our house on the school bus that morning, he had noticed we had a lot of wine bottles in our recycling bin. What!?! I also had a time where a student asked if I would purchase a pregnancy test for her. She said that if she went in and did it her mother would hear about it before she even got back to the school. These are the interesting aspects of small-town living — where people can almost be too connected at times.

In 2015 I decided that life was not hectic enough and I became a real estate agent in addition to being a teacher. At that point I was full-time guidance which meant I was extremely busy during the school day and rarely took a "lunch break" but also meant that I no longer had the marking load of a classroom teacher. This allowed me the flexibility to leave school at the end of the day and do real estate work into the evening and on weekends.

It's funny, they tell you not to say "I'm a real estate agent because I love houses and I love people", but for me it is totally true. I love working with people. In fact, I would say that the great disadvantages of working on my own is the lack of brainstorming and the lack of camaraderie that comes with having a team. I am very hopeful that as more people in my area find out how amazing our brokerage is, they will want to come and join me. I do feel that having a team around me is my happy place to be. Working alone definitely has benefits, but as a very social person I miss the buzz of a busy school setting. I am super thankful though that I get to see so many incredible clients throughout the day, and that my brokerage, although based in Toronto, has a number of zoom meetings throughout the week as this has helped me get to know several agents in our company.

My love of houses developed at a young age. When I was a kid my mom and I would go to local open houses or to new subdivisions and check out the model homes. My mom liked looking at decorating ideas, but I loved the basic design. I think in my next life I may consider being an architect. I enjoy suggesting ways my clients could move a wall or change a layout to make a house work for them. I always find it surprising that this isn't something that comes naturally to other people. I am equally as surprised that it does to me — I certainly can't figure out how to manipulate more than one side of a Rubik's cube!

For my first six years in real estate, I worked with a well-established local agent. I found the real estate courses, although filled with lots of great information, didn't really prepare me for the day to day of the real estate industry. Partnering with a local successful agent was invaluable. I learned so much in a short period of time. I truly believe real estate should incorporate a mandatory internship as part of the licensing process as there is so much value in learning from doing in ways a book can never teach you.

In 2021, I retired from teaching and became a full-time agent. I left my real estate partner and the brokerage I was with and decided to become a solo agent. After interviewing all the local brokerages and some colleagues who worked with these different businesses, I decided to move to Harvey Kalles Real Estate Brokerage. There are two main things that drew me to them. The first is that they believe real estate agents are educators, not salespeople — obviously as a teacher this resonates with me. The second is their philosophy that "every real estate transaction should feel like a luxury experience." To me this is critical. I believe in treating everyone with dignity, respect, and a deep sense of caring. I want the people I work with to know I am invested in their pursuit of housing and that I am looking after their very best interests in the process.

Harvey Kalles is actually a small(ish) boutique brokerage in Toronto, known for dealing with luxury real estate. They have expanded into Haliburton and the Muskokas and opened a brokerage in Picton just for me, which was incredibly kind and generous of them. I love the education they provide for their agents. They have an incredibly supportive staff filled with advisors and a large marketing team who all work alongside me to meet my clients' needs.

I believe my background as an educator sets me apart as a real estate agent in a couple of ways. As a life-long learner it is important to me that I am knowledgeable about all aspects of my role. I read articles about real estate, I seek out and listen to what the experts in my field are saying and I invest in ongoing training for myself. I also study my local market to ensure I am aware of what is happening in my area moment by moment. I am also always trying to educate my clients. I want them to have all the knowledge they need to make wise choices. I try to share my knowledge on social media as well. I have embraced video on platforms such as TikTok, YouTube, and Facebook. I honestly felt so out of my depth at first, but the more you do it the easier it becomes. I still feel very "old" when I scroll on these platforms looking for trending sounds and songs, but if it helps people learn, then hey, I would rather create 10 videos than knock on one stranger's door.

My education background also lends itself to me being known as a patient real estate agent. I always tell people I would rather show them 30 houses and, in the process, have them become knowledgeable and confident in their final decision than have them feel rushed and possibly regret their decision. For most of us, our house is the biggest purchase we will ever make. It is a huge responsibility to be guiding people through this process and I would never be able to sleep at night if I thought I had encouraged someone to make a decision that was not in their best interest. I am in the fortunate position not to need to sell a house to put food on the table, so I am able to really let people take their time to decide what truly works for them. There is no perfect house, but if we can find something that is close to perfect then we can all feel we have made a wise choice.

Country living is different from city living in a myriad of ways. Obvious things like septic systems and wells are foreign entities to people who have previously never had to consider them. So is not having natural gas as a heating option or needing to worry about the trees blocking your internet signal. There are rules about how far from an active barn a house can be built and many other issues that one doesn't have to consider until you are thrust into that situation. Therefore, it is so important to work with a local real estate person who can guide you and help you expand your list of priorities and concerns when looking for a property.

Like any location, Prince Edward County is filled with tiny pockets of sub-communities. It is sometimes easier to work with people who have spent time in the area, so they have a sense of which areas they enjoy the most and want to spend time in. I once spent an entire day driving clients around and taking them out to eat and visit a few local attractions so they could get a better sense of the vastness and uniqueness of The County before they began their search in earnest. Although it is not common these days, one benefit of driving with your clients is the ability to draw their attention to points of interest along the way and ask questions about their needs and wants while driving from location to location.

It is also important to remember that living in an area is much different than visiting an area as a tourist. If you come to The County as a tourist, you will likely be wanting to spend time at the beach, the wineries, or our incredible art studios. You will be less concerned about proximity to a grocery store (we only have four) or gas station (you can be 45 minutes away from one at some of the corners of the County) or the one and only hospital. I had one client couple who thought they wanted to be out in the country until they realized how far it was to their favourite coffee shop — or any coffee shop for that matter, the closest one being a 15-minute drive from where they were looking. That entirely changed their search, and they ended up in a gorgeous century house in town on a large lot that was a five-minute walk to a great coffee spot.

Prince Edward County has been going through its own transition in the form of a slow cultural revolution. Once thought of as a backwards place filled with "hicks" (my uncle, to this day, makes fun of me for living "across the bridge"), it has developed into a vacation hot spot filled with incredible restaurants, wineries, breweries, cideries, and distilleries. It has a wealth of talented artists who call it home as well as a burgeoning number of residents involved in the film industry.

In my short time in real estate, I have seen a change in demographics from people who were wanting to make The County their retirement destination to young 30-somethings looking to escape the city and make their nest egg stretch as far as possible. With an increasing number of people able to work remotely, people are questioning the value of staying in big cities and are looking for a slower pace of life where they can own a house sooner and still be surrounded by a vibrant community. Many are becoming the envy of their friends and family as they can make The County their home base.

As I have the pleasure of working with these individuals, I also get to experience the subtle shifts in the makeup of The County community first-hand. I am seeing who is moving here and the values they are bringing with them. I get to educate them regarding what is important to County residents and how to fit in and find their place here. I remind them that they need to embrace the smell of manure from the fields being fertilized to support the farmers markets they love shopping at, to do the two-finger wave while driving, not to be frustrated when stuck behind a giant combine going 30 km an hour down the two-lane twisty road, and to support the local restaurants and businesses during the winters when there are so many fewer tourists visiting.

I am also able to assist people moving here make connections more quickly. I can give them references to painters, plumbers, and great contractors. I can advise them on local garden centres, farmers markets, and the "secret" beaches. I can also introduce them to their neighbours by throwing them a "welcome to the neighbourhood" party as a closing gift. This I find allows people to quickly become a part of their community. I had a client who purchased a house a few years back. She and her husband were moving here from the Toronto area. They bought their house a couple of years before they planned to move in. It was an adorable house with nice woods across the street. It was perfect for them, and they were thrilled. I helped them find some local renters to fill the gap before they themselves moved in. The funny thing was that once they moved in, the woman started to get antsy. Six months after they moved in, her husband called me and said, "I think we are going to sell the house and move." I was shocked. When I asked why, his wife said there just weren't enough neighbours close to her. She loved the house but really wanted to live where they could have people over and host neighbourhood parties. They ended up selling and moving only a few kms away but into a lovely area that is a small community unto itself where they are much happier.

When I made the transition from teaching to real estate, I moved from what I found to be one of the most trusted and respected jobs to one of the least trusted. I am trying to change that, and I feel connections play a key role in this. If I can use my role as a real estate agent to assist people, not only in moving from one place to another, but in truly getting connected to their community, and if I can be a trusted advisor in this process, then hopefully I can show people that real estate agents care about their clients and about the place where they work and live.

I am thrilled to have partnered with Parkbench. It allows me to give back to my local businesses and not-for-profit organizations as well as assist my clients. As I grow my Parkbench website and continue to add interviews with local businesses and people, I am growing a network of connections that everyone can tap into to find each other more easily and make life not only less stressful, but more enjoyable. After all, our best memories come from the time spent with others.

Prince Edward County is truly a special and exceptional place to live. I am so happy my life transitions have brought me here and I am so proud to assist others and help them make connections as they also make transitions to or within The County.

Suzanne White

REACH OUT TO SUZANNE WHITE

Real Estate Broker with Harvey Kalles Real Estate Ltd., Brokerage - 6 Talbot Street, Picton ON K0K 2T0
Direct Phone Number - 613-921-0481
suzanne@hearthandhavenrealestate.com
https://www.hearthandhavenrealestate.com
Facebook - Hearth and Haven
Instagram - hearthandhavenrealestate
TikTok - hearthandhavenrealestate
LinkedIn - Suzanne White

WHAT CLIENTS ARE SAYING ABOUT SUZANNE

> *"Suzanne knows everything there is to know about real estate in Prince Edward County and surrounding areas. We've successfully purchased three properties through Suzanne and she has been an integral part of our team since the first day we met. With years of experience living and working in the region, Suzanne is not only incredibly informed, but also well-connected to the community. With Suzanne's support, we've explored countless ideas and opportunities together, and she's consistently been responsive, delivered sound advice, and been a true pleasure to work with. We would strongly recommend Suzanne for anyone looking for a local REALTOR®."*

~ Dan F.

"In the spring of 2022 I was looking to enter the housing market and was so fortunate to work with Suzanne White. Suzanne was supportive, encouraging, and professional throughout our search. She was always quick to respond and set up appointments. She provided very sound advice as we looked at multiple properties and presented offers. I could not be happier with the home I purchased thanks to Suzanne. Her knowledge and ability to navigate all aspects, from the initial stages of searching, to ensuring everything was in place after moving in was exceptional. I highly recommend Suzanne White for anyone looking to buy or sell - you will be in the very best of hands!"

~ Heather M.

"With her guidance and expertise, we have purchased two homes and sold one in Prince Edward County. Suzanne is well grounded in the County and has a myriad of useful contacts to support the home improvements that her clients may require."

~ Rachael W.

CHAPTER 12

3 PERCENT REALTY REVOLUTION, INC.

" Our values are what ultimately led us to 3% Realty. The franchisors understand what we are trying to accomplish and are very supportive of our efforts. Now that we have set up the foundation of our business, we are starting to recruit people to our team. As we add agents, our idea is to hire according to who they are versus what kind of numbers they bring in."

Tom & Zita Scozzari
Cape Cod, MA

GET TO KNOW TOM & ZITA SCOZZARI

Zita Scozzari is a detail-oriented professional with extensive leadership experience that includes analyzing and enhancing businesses for growth, realigning business processes, and developing products and services. She has a strong background as a project manager and change leader. Zita has directed the efforts of both large and small teams in various industries. She has been recognized for leadership skills, high-energy work ethic, communication, and dedication to teamwork. As a real estate professional, Zita possesses the knowledge and experience needed to guide clients smoothly through the home buying and selling process.

Tom Scozzari stands at the forefront of business owner asset preservation. He has spent the past three decades dedicated to helping building owners manage their property and energy costs through ever-improving HVAC products. Tom is a calculated risk taker, entrepreneur, and visionary. Zita and Tom have years of partnership success and look forward to growing teams of real estate professionals on Cape Cod, the Islands, and the South Shore of MA.

3 PERCENT REALTY REVOLUTION, INC.

TOM & ZITA SCOZZARI

We are blessed to live in a part of the world that most people can only dream about visiting. Cape Cod, Nantucket and Martha's Vineyard are our backyard wonderlands. Miles of white powdered sandy beaches line our state along the Cape Cod Bay and Atlantic Ocean. The lush marshes are filled with birds and wildlife that will keep your binoculars glued to your eyes.

The Cape Cod architecture style of home is as American as apple pie. Dating back to New England during the 17th century, this classic style is often replicated in other parts of the country due to its majestic design. New homes are still being built to these specifications, centuries later.

Picture this: *You are riding your bike on the Shining Sea Bikeway with a light breeze cooling your skin. You stop to take pictures of the stacked stone monuments along the beach and then continue your ride to Wood's Hole where you stop for lunch at a local seafood restaurant and savor the catch of the day. As the sun hits its highest point, you take to the waters to cool off or enjoy a whale watching tour. As the sun begins to set, your camera is poised to capture the beauty of the area — no filter required.* That's Cape Cod in a snapshot!

CLAM SHACKS AND LOBSTER ROLLS

Tom grew up on Cape Cod and I [Zita] came from Maine and deciding to settle here was like a homecoming for us. With 15 towns on the Cape, each one is a little different from the next. Some are true coastal havens, others have more history, and some have more of an eclectic vibe, but regardless of which direction you choose, it will be a special experience. A mere 65 miles long and at most, 20 miles wide, it is easy to get around to any of these unique communities.

Going to the local clam shack — so Tom can eat his favorite fried clam sandwich and I can devour a good lobster roll — tops our list of favorite eats in the area. People from all over the world come to visit, which adds more flavor to these parts. We can't say enough about our home.

As a business consultant, I traveled extensively for many years. Although I loved my job, I knew at some point I wanted to be back home with Tom and my family. The catalyst that led me into real estate was the COVID-19 pandemic. I was grounded from traveling and was looking for a new direction. Little did I know, Tom had been praying for me to be home. I still think that causing the pandemic was a little much, Tom!

As a franchise consultant, I [Tom] came across the 3% Realty franchise and was quite impressed by the systems of operation, as well as the opportunities that it presented for us. We couldn't argue with the numbers as we realized the reduction in commissions can lead to a large amount of savings for the seller and potentially the buyer as well.

One agent, Jennifer Kibler, helped change our perspective on what agents can and should do. Up until that point, the main focus around buying or selling was trying to minimize cost and agent commissions. We knew instinctively there had to be a better way and Jennifer showed us that path. As we head into this journey it is our goal to help train, mentor, and support more "Jennifers" — well-trained, full-service agents, but for a more competitive listing fee.

We have a goal of building teams across Massachusetts who are not only great at their chosen profession, but who also give back to their communities. We have always given a tithe to our church and more to various charities, but we want to give more and have a plan to increase the amount and percentage we give as our business grows.

WHAT I LOVE, LOVE, LOVE

As a real estate agent, I [Zita] love just about every aspect of the business. Topping my list are the life stories my clients share with me. I learn so much through these relationships and want more of them!

More examples of why I love this business:

- Each day is something new.
- I never stop learning.
- Other real estate agents are interesting and have unique stories of their own. I get to meet and work with them daily.
- It's a chance to do some good.
- I can let my freedom flag fly — I can be me!
- I get to be a detective and solve problems.

To add, I [Tom] prefer new construction homes and Zita is drawn to vintage homes, so we've experienced that "challenge" created when partners in life have different desires. This perspective enables us to embrace the question: "What house will we find that they will agree on? It starts as a mystery, but you get to help solve it . . . and always do! Solving mysteries is one of the more fun things we do.

Building teams is what we do best. Between our franchise and the use of the Parkbench platform, our future team members will be able to leverage these models to their advantage. We want to help them be successful in any way we can, and we think Parkbench is perfect for that. Getting out in the community, meeting new people, and getting referrals is all part of the process and Parkbench fits squarely into our business process.

Helping small businesses with video marketing on a 'free-to-them' basis, is a component of our brand we want to accentuate. It really creates a lot of additional goodwill.

3% REALTY REVOLUTION

Relationships are at the heart of our business. Tom is a mastermind of knowledge and is a great source of information for our clients. I have a heart for the homeless and veterans due in part because my dad is a veteran. The thought of veterans not having a home breaks my heart.

I also have a soft spot for single moms without moms. These women have not had the good fortune of being loved and nourished by their own moms. They struggle with balancing accounts and day to day living. As a mother of three, I know love and nurturing are part of being healthy, both mentally and spiritually. If we can effect change for families, we can change a generation of people caught in the cycle of homelessness.

As parents to three wonderful children and 25 amazing grandkids, we take nothing for granted. We have a community within a community — you should see us at Thanksgiving! Family and friends are at the core of our lives and livelihoods.

Our values are what ultimately led us to 3% Realty. The franchisors understand what we are trying to accomplish and are very supportive of our efforts. Now that we have set up the foundation of our business, we are starting to recruit people to our team. As we add agents, our idea is to hire according to who they are versus what kind of numbers they bring in. Caring for and knowing our community is high on our list when considering bringing someone on.

In terms of what we can offer other agents, it starts and ends with a full-service package. We tap into the franchise model for resources and support, and the agents receive unlimited access to these systems. Furthermore, we provide hands-on training and mentorship. The advertising, websites (including Parkbench), and social media platforms, are available to everyone to capitalize on.

We really want to create a new and revolutionary way of selling real estate! Our goal is to keep overhead low so we can offer full service to our sellers at a reduced rate: 3% versus the normal 6% of the sale. If you look at the graph below you will see that selling a $600,000 home will save a seller $18,000. We are confident they can find something worthwhile to do with that money.

Building something which will live long past our days is exciting. Who knows, maybe we have 25 new recruits in our midst, once they are out of diapers of course!

I DON'T NEED GOOGLE

My wife, Zita is a genius! She is one of the smartest people I know. Her intelligence level and her ability to work with people are fabulous. In a nutshell: *"I don't need Google; my wife knows everything!"*

One reason I love working with Zita is she doesn't forget, unless I've done something terrible, but even then, she has the class to not bring things up again! We are best buddies, true soulmates, and feel like we've known each other since the beginning of time. Every day, we draw closer to each other. I couldn't imagine spending my life (or workday) with anyone else!

When Tom and I met I was a shy, introverted girl from Maine, but Tom has always been my courage. He has absolutely no fear, so when he tells me I can do anything I believe him. I have had several successful careers and so much of that I attribute to Tom's loving encouragement. He is filled with courage, ambition, and a strong desire to succeed, but he also truly cares about people. He makes every day an adventure and it's fun to do life with him.

In the end, we are a really good team as we have weathered our fair share of ups and downs throughout our journey together.

FIXER UPPERS, LADDERS, AND A CREDIT CARD

We are very grateful for the past challenges we have faced, because without them we would not be here today. In 2008, we watched our property investments evaporate before our eyes, due to the recession we were facing. Of course, we had to pivot and rebuild from there.

Zita and I bought our first house with a credit card for $18,000. It was a bank foreclosure that needed a lot of tender loving care. We had a camper parked in the backyard and we lived in these tight quarters with our kids during the renovations. I accidentally backed my Jeep into the septic tank which proceeded to swallow it up. We took so much garbage out that the dumpster was bigger than the house!

Once we completed all the renovations and repairs, Zita looked at me and said, "We are moving. We are in the wrong school district." I felt like I was going to pass out!

We have owned one of our current homes for 17 years. It was still in a state of demo/renovation as I [Tom] forgot I had to put it all together after I took it all apart. For example, Zita was climbing down a ladder from our bedroom in high heels when she stated, "Tom, we are moving!" I guess I forgot about the stairs too! The house is now fully renovated and is part of our love story, which is probably why we cannot seem to let it go.

We love fixer uppers and love the experiences we have had in each of our houses. One of my [Zita] favorites was a large, yellow brick house in the center of town. Once we began working on it, we would have people stop by and thank us for taking care of it because it had historical value to the neighborhood. Once owned by a cigar manufacturer, this house hosted many parties for the community residents, and we carried on the tradition.

This reminds me [Zita] of my daughter's 16th birthday party when we had a band playing music and the dancing spilled into the streets. Danielle, the birthday girl, took candy to the children dancing to the music. It was a magical time.

THE FRANCHISE EXPERIENCE

As we grow and expand our own team, we are also focusing on recruiting for the franchise. The main areas we are concentrating on are New England, especially Boston. However, we can help agents anywhere across the country get involved in the franchise.

The process begins with a psychological assessment to determine your attributes and to see if you would be a good fit for 3 Percent Realty US. We can jump in and offer insight for people as they work through the process. I [Tom] can further help by gaining an understanding of your goals to see if they align with those of the franchise.

This isn't our first step into the franchise world as we have also been involved in Kumon Learning, Travel Host, GarageTek, and Anytime Fitness. We believe in systems because they work, and our experience only adds to the foundation of what we are building.

LEAVING A LEGACY

We have been involved in real estate for the better part of our lives. Simply put, we love houses! We are dedicated to creating something larger than ourselves and hope to leave our family a business they can take over and call their own someday.

Thank you, Roy and Gavin, of 3% Realty for entrusting us with your brand; we will do you proud.

We want to thank Jennifer Kibler, the best agent we have ever worked with. She renewed our faith in the real estate industry.

My [Tom] brother, Tim, thank you for your guidance and patience. We are inspired by you and your successful real estate career of 16 years and counting.

Our parents have been our sounding boards, supporters, and often our biggest fans. We wouldn't be here without you and love you very much!

Our children and grandchildren have made us so proud. We love watching you become such loving and caring people. Thank you for being our support when we needed it most. We love you all!

Zita & Tom

REACH OUT TO TOM & ZITA SCOZZARI

Website: https://parkbench.com/cape-cod
Phone: (508) 321-SOLD

CHAPTER 13

A VOICE FOR RENTON

" For me, keeping things real and following my heart keeps me in the driver's seat."

Tanya Barrans
Renton, WA

GET TO KNOW TANYA BARRANS

A native Pacific Northwesterner, Tanya Barrans is an outgoing, giving, and exceptional real estate professional serving King, Pierce, and Snohomish Counties.

Tanya began her real estate journey in 2019. She started thinking about becoming a licensed realtor after a conversation with a friend, and once she realized the desire wasn't going away, she did her 90 clock hours in nine days, got her license, and never looked back! She is proud to have had over 60 transactions and $30M in total sales since then. In that time, she also received the Best of Zillow Award and the Top Agent Award from Homesnap.

Passion for her clients is what drives Tanya's day-to-day business. There is nothing more exciting than finding the perfect property for someone. She gets so invested that a popular joke with her clients is that you'd think she was moving in, too! The adrenaline rush that comes with submitting a bid that beats out all the competition is unparalleled.

A VOICE FOR RENTON

TANYA BARRANS

Born and raised as a Pacific Northwest native, I call Renton, Washington my home. I have lived in many different parts of the state, but I always find my way back.

Renton used to be considered the 'ghetto' suburb and it took people a long time to change their mindset, although some people still haven't. It has a quaint feel to it and the locals love the old school, vintage restaurants we have, particularly the *'Melrose Steakhouse'* — reservations required!

Our historic downtown, although currently being revitalized, has a few 'left-over' feels from its late 1800s beginnings. You will love the new retail shops mixed in with the nostalgic history of this town. While strolling down main street with a steaming hot coffee and a handmade cupcake you can decide to go to the arcade or maybe the gardening shop, without having to hop into a cab!

In contrast, *'The Landing'* is becoming the hub of Renton. Its *shop, dine, play* brand is at the heart of this new development. I'm excited to see how this will complement the old, small town that I grew up in.

The neighboring city of Bellevue has essentially been priced out of the market and that's, in part, why Renton is growing exponentially.

This is also a big reason why Renton has been focusing on revitalization and is increasing its infrastructure in expectation of more growth.

Since the effects of the Covid-19 pandemic, many people have been working from home and are finding Renton a great place that is also affordable. The county wasn't capitalizing on the livable and buildable land it had, until recently. We now have the Seattle Seahawks training facility here; Top Golf has also moved in, and the Sounders training facility is coming soon. The Hyatt on the Water is a new hotel built on Lake Washington which is a beautiful addition to our area.

COOKIES

If you are considering making a move here, you are in for a nice surprise. Renton is considered a commuter city and the airport is a quick 20-minute drive. It is smack dab in the middle of Seattle, Bellevue, and Tacoma, making it centrally located to all the action!

When I moved into my current home, I got cookies from the neighbors and 'sweet Jane' and Denver, her husband, keep a watchful eye out for partiers and strangers lurking around! I have lived in places where I never even knew my neighbors' names, let alone getting cookies from them! I love it!

Speaking of cookies, there aren't many cookie-cutter homes here. Every home is different from the next, which adds a lot of value to the landscape. Due to the influx of young people and a large immigrant population, we are considered a little melting pot of sorts. I have worked with countless people who come from different countries, and I am thought of as a transition or relocation expert in these parts. I love working with Pacific Northwest (PNW) transplants as I learn so much about where they came from and what their dreams are when they come here.

DOING IT ON MY OWN

I grew up in an upper middle-class neighborhood which I wasn't comfortable with from a young age. I associated being rich with being fake and shallow — which I was neither. I spent a lot of time growing up in my church youth group in Renton. At church, I felt more myself and connected with those friends easier. I liked the down-to-earth vibe they had, and I was able to be myself with them. However, I remember a time when I was doing a mission trip with my church to an orphanage in Mexico. I overheard a friend describe me as, "Tanya's so rich, she has a big house," to one of older kids in the orphanage. I was so embarrassed and did not want this kid to feel less than because of his life circumstances. From that moment on, I wanted to hide where I came from so no one ever felt that I was above them. I became very passionate about helping others in need and hoping I could partner with them to achieve any dream they had.

As the years went on, I developed a new relationship with money. It's no longer that money is wrong but what you do with it matters. A slogan I adopted many years back is, "if you think you make enough money, your purpose isn't big enough!" I have carried that through for the last decade and strive to always find ways I can give back to my friends, causes, and community.

These experiences have helped me create a passion for Renton. It's the place that accepted me for me and where I developed into the person I am today. Renton, as a community, is also trying to develop into who it is. I have always believed Renton has so much to offer but it wasn't always seen that way. Just like I like to help others, I realized I want to be a voice for Renton, too and help others see just how wonderful of a town it is!

I started my career as a salesperson when I was 14, working the phone lines, or in the 'sweat shop' as I prefer to call it. I knew at that time I was destined to be in sales of some sort. I actually dabbled in real estate in 2008 but it was a disaster. I found myself driving to Tacoma in the dark in the middle of winter thinking to myself, *"I will never do this again!"*

Fast forward 10 years, after returning from maternity leave, I was laid off. As the sole breadwinner of my family, this was a shock and I had to pivot quickly. I interviewed everywhere and at the end of each interview I was told the same thing; "You were great, but '*Bob*' works here already, and he is getting it." It was the same broken record, one story after another.

I had a brief conversation with some friends who thought I should try real estate again. Hmmmmm, really? I interviewed with a big real estate brokerage and then decided I would get my license and give it another try. As I was preparing, I had four people tell me, *"Oh I would have used you to sell/buy our house if I knew you were getting your license."* Not wanting to miss out on any other deals, I went into turbo mode and got my required 90 clock hours done in nine days!

I stopped interviewing for jobs and headed straight into it. I had to prove to myself I could do it, without my pride taking another hit. I joined a bunch of mom groups and met a woman in need of my services. Within three weeks she was under contract — I made my first sale!

I signed up with Zillow to send me leads and I was told, *"Pick up every time your phone rings — that's what you have to do."* My first experience was memorable, to say the least. I woke up to my first Zillow call at 8:00 am on a Sunday, from a prospective client who wanted to buy a house. I didn't know what to expect from Zillow leads but it had to be better than the $300 dollars I had spent on flyers, without a call. Zillow was game-changing to help launch my career as it gave me the experience and confidence I needed, as a new agent.

After about two and a half years, I grew tired of the Sunday dinner calls from people wanting to see houses within the hour. I dropped my Zillow service as it was no longer serving me well. I wanted to continue to build my contacts and connections on a more personal level and invest more in my community.

TIME TO RESET

Six months after I got my license, my husband and I separated, and I became a single mom. I am always reflective and appreciative of how God saw what I could not. God knew I would need a career that would allow me to provide for my son but also gave me the flexibility to spend quality time with him as well, especially during his early, formative years. My career was in full swing over the summer of 2020, and I was closing a transaction every week or two.

In late 2020, I reconnected with a childhood friend, Travis, who showed me what real love was and encouraged me to shine. With the gain in my self-confidence, I was able to achieve new heights in my career. I went back to school full-time and decided to become a managing broker and start a team.

In full transparency, Travis and I were both actively involved in Alcoholics Anonymous (AA). AA and recovery are huge passions of mine and something I take very seriously. I would not be where I am today in my career and motherhood, if not for this program. Our epic love story was cut short when Travis lost his battle to addiction and died in May of 2022. My passion for recovery is now stronger than ever and helping others not have the same fate as Travis.

I recently celebrated one year in my sobriety in 2022 and I'm not looking in the rearview mirror! The last three years have been some of the best and worst years of my life.

THE RIGHT TIME

I know that God has set a plan for me, and I am taking some positive steps towards making my life better. I am super involved in AA, and I am often invited to speak openly about addiction and rehab, all in an effort to help others.

Parkbench came along at exactly the right time in my career. It is forcing me to get out there and become an advocate and use my voice to a higher level. I'm wanting to be the 'Renton expert' for my community. I mean, why not? I was born and raised here, I know every square inch of my town and I am an advocate for change. I want my name to be synonymous with Renton, not necessarily the best real estate agent but the best go-to person. I want them to say, *"Talk to Tanya, she will know someone who can help you with that."*

As I am doing more interviews, I am meeting more people who have shared with me their personal addiction and recovery stories. It is so heartwarming to know that this marketing platform is more than a website URL; instead it's a vehicle for me to make these important life-altering connections.

UNAPOLOGETICALLY ME

As a team leader, I have been manifesting my team to be diverse, approachable, and authentic. I have one teammate who was worried about having too many tattoos and he wasn't sure if he would look professional enough to work in real estate. My answer to this was, I want people to look at us and say, "I look like them, I talk like they do, and I can relate to them."

We will attract people because of our diversity so I don't worry about those who will shy away from us. I am unapologetically me, so get used to it!

I have some big goals and dreams to fulfill. I'd like to create a scholarship fund for people entering recovery treatment and my even bigger dream is to have a dream center for the people of Renton to enjoy. These purposes drive me every single day.

KEEP IT REAL

Having been in the real estate industry for some time now there are definitely things I would have changed and others I would not have touched. For someone thinking about getting into the real estate business, here are some things I would recommend:

- Get organized.
- Set boundaries or you might burn out.
- Schedule days off.
- Post everything you do in a day; it shows your level of commitment.
- Manage your social media.
- Analyze your budget.
- Niche your area of expertise.

I wouldn't recommend:

- Trying to be everything to everyone.
- Sending out mailers without intention.
- Driving two hours to show a house.
- Picking 20 things to do in a day — you won't get anything done.

For me, keeping things real and following my heart keeps me in the driver's seat.

"YOU GOT THIS BABE"

As I take a moment to reflect on my life's journey, I can't help but feel an immense amount of gratitude towards the people who have supported me throughout. I am truly blessed to have so many people by my side. Thank you all, I truly would not be who I am today without every one of you.

I want to thank you, Travis. As we began our journey together, you taught me so much about love and life. You always encouraged me to believe in myself and chase my wild dreams. Now, as I move on to new love, new ambitions, and new adventures, I still carry with me your spirit and hear you saying, "You got this babe".

> *Travis, before you, I didn't know a love like this could exist. I didn't know relationships could be this easy, comfortable, and fun. I didn't know you could look at your partner on day 600 with more love and attraction than on day one. But you changed all that for me. The way you would look at me, treat me, value me, and believe in me was like nothing I have ever experienced before. You gave me freedom to be me. You loved me for my crazy past, and you cheered me on for my wild dreams for the future. Every time I'd get overwhelmed with work or school, you'd say, "Babe, stop overanalyzing, you got this." And then I'd get it. And you'd laugh and say, "Duh babe, I told you." Even as I'm writing this, I'm smiling and feeling you with me. Saying, babe you got this, everyone will love what you say. Geez, I could cry right now since I feel your spirit with me so much.*

One of my favorite poems recently came across my path and I will end with this…

"...then one day, I looked into the mirror and said, 'Wow. After all the hurts, bruises, and everything I've been through, I made it. I survived, and I'm stronger.' So, I have straightened my crown and I walk away, ***like a boss."***

Tanya Barrans

REACH OUT TO TANYA BARRANS

Tanya Barrans Group
https://www.tanyabarransgroup.com
https://www.facebook.com/tanyabarrans
https://www.youtube.com/channel/UCtGgw7DWOnmI_AjT2Sj8V2g
https://www.tanyabarransgroup.com/www.instagram.com/tanyabarrans

WHAT CLIENTS ARE SAYING ABOUT TANYA

"Tanya is an amazing real estate agent, but, more importantly, an amazing person. She is a genuinely kind and caring human being, and a total gem. My husband and I stumbled across her by chance on Zillow, and we are so, so grateful we did! She went out of her way to help us find homes and make sure we understood everything. Home-buying is never an easy experience, especially in a seller's market, but Tanya made it all worth it and helped get us through some really disappointing and stressful times. Count yourself lucky if you get to work with her!!!!"

~Carolyn B.

"Tanya is by far the best real estate agent that we have worked with! After working with a different agent for four months with no success, we decided to reach out to Tanya. We asked her to help us find a house. We gave her only a week. She helped us find the perfect house in the right neighborhood in 4 days! Tanya is compassionate and knowledgeable about the housing market. Not

only does Tanya take her job very seriously, but she has her clients' best interest at heart. We already consider her a friend and highly recommend her to anyone who is looking to buy and/or sell a house."

~Bernice M.

"We met Tanya early in our house search process and she stuck with us even as we changed our search area. She always went the extra mile to help us try to make the most competitive offer possible, including gathering extra information or touring the house multiple times with us. With her help our offer was accepted on a five bedroom/three bath dream house for our family, even with multiple other competitive offers. The closing process was very smooth, and we couldn't be happier with the care she showed throughout the process, even checking in after we closed. Highly recommend."

~Lisa P.

"Tanya is an AMAZING Realtor®. She is knowledgeable, responsive, reliable, encouraging.... we could go on and on. Only a few years from retirement, we weren't planning to buy another home. We have a beautiful retirement home waiting for us. But a job opportunity presented itself that couldn't be passed up and we found ourselves scrambling to buy a second home. Tanya worked hard to get us a great house at a great price. A year later, she is still checking on us and treating us like family. She's the best!"

~Kara R.

CHAPTER 14

A SUBSCRIPTION TO HUMAN NATURE

" In my opinion, real estate is a combination of both art and science. Most people want a fair market value for their house, and they don't want to play games. The end goal is someone wants to sell their house, and someone wants to buy it, so we should be able to figure it out."

Scott Fishman
Evanston, IL

GET TO KNOW SCOTT FISHMAN

Representing homeowners and future homeowners, in Evanston, Skokie, Park Ridge, Rogers Park, Andersonville, or Lincoln Square, Scott brings his knowledge and experience to his clients to ensure their real estate process is easy. Scott is a lifetime Chicagoan, a DePaul graduate with degrees in History and Public Administration. After teaching high school social studies, Scott made a career shift to advertising and PR. Working on a variety of global brands, Scott spent over 20 years helping his clients tell their story through design, advertising, public relations, and on-line communications. Knowing it was time for a new chapter, Scott earned his real estate license and went to work helping his clients navigate their path to home ownership.

As the Principal of The Fishman Group, Scott and his team focus on clear communication with their clients and all parties involved in the deal. Educating clients about the home buying and selling process, recommending other industry experts, and making sure every detail is understood, is critical to the service that The Fishman Group provides. When Scott is not working with his clients, he is spending time with his wife Jenny, his kids Patrick, Eve, and Nate, coaching baseball, playing drums with a number of local bands, and serving on several nonprofit and community boards.

A SUBSCRIPTION TO HUMAN NATURE

SCOTT FISHMAN

Evanston is a town of about 85,000 and it is the first community north of Chicago. It's about as close as you can get to Chicago without actually being in Chicago. Northwestern University is located here, and it helped put Evanston on the map. We are right on the shoreline of Lake Michigan, which is a bonus too.

My family and I moved here about seven years ago from Chicago. I grew up in the south suburbs and went to school at DePaul University in the city. I spent most of my adult life living in Chicago, and it's where I met my wife, Jenny. We made the move to Evanston due in part to the school system here. Our daughter was entering middle school and the public school system in Chicago required selective enrollment which means one has to test into them. We simply did not want our kids to have to be anxious or worry about what school they would attend.

It's easy to live here. I love that we can get anywhere in any direction to any destination within 20 minutes. My son can ride his bike to his baseball games which he wouldn't have been able to do otherwise. Evanston has everything to offer that the big city does, just on a smaller scale.

We have a host of local micro breweries like Sketchbook, Temperance, and Smilie Brothers which have become really popular in the last few years. I personally like to work from coffee shops, and I have some great choices such as Brothers K, Backlot, or Hoosier Mama's Pie Shop.

MID-WESTERN MIND-SET

The real estate market here is quite typical of the rest of the country. The last two years have been met with a crazy frenzy of activity — mainly people panicking to buy which results in over-priced properties and disappointed buying clients. Single family homes are still in demand although the inventory remains too low.

With the recent increase of interest rates to help combat inflation and a potential recession, I am looking forward to a more balanced market. A balanced market takes the leveraging component out of the equation and leaves a more desirable negotiating platform. Honestly, it weeds out a lot of the bad Realtors® because real estate is more than just putting a for sale sign up and filling out the paperwork.

In my opinion, real estate is a combination of both art and science. Most people want a fair market value for their house, and they don't want to play games. The end goal is someone wants to sell their house, and someone wants to buy it, so we should be able to figure it out. My belief is if a house is worth $400,000 then it should sell for $400,000 — give or take a few thousand on either side. Waiving rights as a buyer by either going way over price, waving inspections, or even waving their mortgage contingencies is not in anyone's best interest and I advise my clients against it.

Chicagoans have a reputation for having a 'Midwestern mentality' and by this I am referring to being moderate people with a sense of fair play. We are not used to waiving all our negotiating powers. My approach is more about a fair deal and making it reasonable for all parties.

A MORAL COMPASS

Real estate was not my first gig, but it is likely to be my last one. I had a 20-year career in the advertising industry and worked for some large

PR firms in the Chicago area. The entrepreneurial spirit led me to open my own small marketing firm, unfortunately just before the 2008 recession. A good friend of mine and client, who was a real estate agent, was needing help and I was hitting a brick wall in terms of wanting to get out of the advertising industry.

I took an intensive two-week real estate course and obtained my state license and began my new journey. I started at the same office as my friend Jayne, and she was incredibly generous with her time and support. She gave me all sorts of leads and open houses to get me going as a new agent.

She taught me the 'right' way to conduct business. Having a moral compass in an industry that can be morally bankrupt set me in the direction I wanted to go. I can't even imagine what could have happened if I didn't have a mentor like Jayne supporting me. This is what motivated me as a team leader.

RELATIONSHIPS ARE KEY

Getting to know my clients is a critical step in building trust between us. I prefer to meet for coffee with a potential client so I can get a sense whether we will be a good fit to work together. This allows me to focus on their needs, goals, and questions without the distraction of showing a house at the same time.

I like to have a good working relationship with other agents, so deals can run smoothly, and the two parties can be more honest with each other. Ultimately, my clients will be better served when these relationships are established.

One thing that blew me away when I first started was the referral fees I received when I sent a client to another agent in another city. I found this to be more than generous, as this was virtually unheard of in corporate America.

DEVELOPING A THICK SKIN

My dad was integral in shaping how I view the business world. He was involved in retail most of his adult life and taught me how and why to develop a thick skin to 'survive' in the corporate atmosphere. "Never ask someone to do something you are not prepared to do yourself," was one of his guiding principles.

Coming into real estate from the advertising world was a breath of fresh air. I was often told I would meet some challenging people in real estate but to this day, I have yet to meet 'crazy' the way I did in advertising. In advertising what was considered an emergency was when a client is arguing over a shade of gray in their ad when it is running in a newspaper.

Coaching has always been an important part of why I am good under pressure. Learning skills that will lead you to be a better listener ultimately pays off in dividends. I describe my style as 'politely blunt' which is well received by people as they know where they stand with me. "I don't want to sell you anything," is my typical approach because I really don't. What I do want is a mutually respectful relationship with my clients. Plain and simple.

I'm not afraid to challenge 'red flags' when they come along. Thankfully, this hasn't happened often, but I will say this, "I don't tolerate racism or discrimination of any kind and I'd rather give up a client than sacrifice my morals and values." My real estate teacher taught me two very valuable lessons that I practice to this day:

- Talk about property and not people.
- Don't practice law.

THE LEARNING CURVE

Changing careers later in life is often met with its own set of challenges. I had to learn a whole new set of skills in an industry that was foreign to me. As an agent, you are on your own to run your business. Like many self-employed careers, there is a lot of on-the-job training.

An ongoing challenge that many agents face is that it is a lonely business as much of the work is done in a vacuum. At the end of the day, it's just you on that island and you have to make it work.

BUT it also makes me stronger and makes me a better agent. Because of my background in advertising and as a small business owner, I'm more approachable with people and I do not want to complicate the process any more than needed. Believe me, someone else will do that for us so let's not be those people!

I CARE ABOUT HUMAN CONNECTION

I've made a conscious decision to spend my time and money on building my sphere of influence. My process includes reaching out to people who know me from other areas of my life. In particular, people whom I used to work with or coached their kids or past clients, etc. I'm getting very intentional with the quality of my sphere of influence vs the sheer number of people in my database.

This is what led me to Parkbench where I meet and interview local business owners and people of influence in my community. Anything that can lead me to human connection — I'm all in! I'm looking forward to the Universe converting my connections into clients.

My sense of community is strong, and I shape my business around values that coincide with my own. When I have a listing client, I want to know more about their home than three beds/ two baths. I want to create a story beyond the pictures and descriptions. I ask such questions as:

- What do you like about living here?
- Why did you choose this neighborhood to live in?
- What makes your home special that people would want to learn about?

I want to be the differentiator in my industry by working within my community to support people within the experience, not just a transaction.

GET INVOLVED

Community is very important to me, which is why my work as a Realtor® is more personal and relationship based and not just a transaction. I love to be involved in community organizations. I coached my son's baseball team for years and was involved in the PTA at our kids' middle school.

I currently sit on the board for *Housing Opportunities for Women* (HOW). It is an organization which helps women at high risk. The core to its existence is to help break the cycle of poverty and homelessness. I am honored to be a board member of their organization.

I am also active on the board of directors for the *Police Oversight Board* in Evanston. It is a very progressive program where citizens review complaints made against the police department. It provides much needed checks and balances and brings a higher level of accountability into the department.

WHAT WOULD JAYNE DO?

As I close off, there are so many people I would like to thank who have helped and encouraged me along the way.

Jayne Alofs encouraged me to become a realtor. She was a great friend and a huge part of my business. She was a good benchmark person as people would often ask, "What would Jayne do?" Our approach to work was very similar and I hope one day I can be half as respected in the community as she was. She sadly passed away far too young. Her clients loved her. I loved her. Rest in Peace.

My wife and #1 fan, Jenny, has been my rock and supported me throughout my career change. She puts up with my seasonal neurosis about the market being slow and my constant mumblings about threatening to work as a barista somewhere!

Thank you, kids: Eve, Nate, and Patrick, for your patience while I dragged you to open houses and showings.

Thank you to all my past and present clients. I enjoy you and let's go for a coffee or beer (or two)!

My team at Compass, I thank you for all your hard work and support.

Scott Fishman

REACH OUT TO SCOTT FISHMAN

Principal, Fishman Group
Licensed Real Estate Salesperson
Worth Clark Real Estate
m: 773.316.5409
scott@fishmangroup.properties
www.fishmangroup.properties

WHAT CLIENTS ARE SAYING ABOUT SCOTT

"Scott is an experienced and savvy Realtor®. He immediately understood our wish list and budget, and the links to potential homes that he sent us were spot on. He responds to emails and texts in real time. I think his phone might be glued to his hand. ;-) He listened sincerely to our feedback on homes we visited, without pushing us to make an offer before we were ready. When we found a home we liked, Scott was very responsive and helped us negotiate a strong (and winning!) offer despite being in a multiple offer situation. On the selling side, Scott's ideas for minor updates to make to the home to get ready to list were really helpful — the house looked so different after the simple changes he suggested. He communicates honestly and non-judgmentally (We definitely ran into some realtors who were the opposite!) Scott was also very open to feedback. He and his team worked extremely hard to maintain a strong open house presence and accommodate showing requests with speed and flexibility. After 6 weeks, we had multiple offers and came in very close to the list price. You are in very good hands with Scott!"

~Altesse

"Working with Scott was a real pleasure. He's professional, on time, answered all my questions, and showed homes that were what I was looking for. He made the homebuying process smooth and had great recommendations for other professionals I needed to purchase my new home. I highly recommend Scott and appreciate all his help."

~Clint F.

"Scott was great to work with both on the sale of our condo and the purchase of our new home. We really appreciated how attentive and responsive he was throughout the process. He had excellent recommendations for the rest of our team and really put in a lot of effort to make sure things went as smoothly as possible, despite many hiccups on the seller's side of our home purchase. We

were able to sell our condo for $21k over list and we purchased our new home for $20k under list thanks to his advice and negotiating skills. Would definitely recommend him, and Compass, to anyone."

~John and Shanna

CHAPTER 15

MAKE TWO DRINKS WELL

"Community comes first. People come first. I consider myself a connector at heart. This role charges my energy every day and allows me to form and grow my sphere of influence. I have resources, knowledge and information that is valuable to people, and I have no problem sharing it all. It simply makes me feel good to be the conduit that makes things happen!"

Anthony Beharry
Columbia, MD

GET TO KNOW ANTHONY BEHARRY

My name is Anthony Beharry, and since becoming licensed in 2003, I have worked in all areas of Real Estate throughout the Washington DC Metropolitan Area. I have represented sellers and buyers, landlords and tenants, investors, and financial institutions. Most of my work has been in Washington DC; Prince Georges County; Howard County, MD; Anne Arundel County, MD; and Montgomery County, MD. In cities such as South Laurel MD, Greenbelt MD, Hillandale MD, North Laurel MD, Bowie MD, Severn MD, Hillcrest Heights MD, Glenn Dale MD, White Oak MD, Beltsville MD, Odenton MD, College Park MD, Fairland MD, Colesville MD, New Carrollton MD, and the surrounding areas.

Although I specialize in working with pre-foreclosures, I have expertise in many areas of real estate. These areas include wholesaling, purchasing, and renovating undervalued residential and commercial real estate, raising money in private capital, converting homes into condominiums, renting residential and commercial properties for cash flow and appreciation, and purchasing non-performing debt instruments. Since 2002, I have completed over 200 real estate projects, earning millions of dollars, and currently controlling millions in assets around the DC metro area.

MAKE TWO DRINKS WELL

ANTHONY BEHARRY

INTRODUCTION

I've lived in Kings Contrivance for a little over a year, but it is the first place I can truly call home. The community here has been so welcoming to my family and me; we know many of our neighbors. One of my favorite things to do is invite our neighbors over to our house for a good old fashioned BBQ cookout.

A fun fact about my city is it is rated the #18 best city to live in America. It was a 'purpose-built' community back in the 1970s which in this case, meant that each neighborhood was self-contained. Independent commercial properties were built to support each area with residential housing surrounding. Ten villages comprise the greater city of Columbia. Nestled between Washington and Baltimore, our city is rich in diversity and culture.

Kings Contrivance is well known for its highly rated, best-in-state schools. This is one of many driving forces that lead people to want to live here. The real estate market is quite dynamic in nature as many original homeowners are now downsizing, replaced by young families.

MY JOURNEY INTO REAL ESTATE

My career began in 1995 but it was far from what I am doing today. I left my home in New York City and attended Howard University in Washington DC, where I studied Mechanical Engineering. After a couple of years, I ran out of money and kicked around for a while. My young, restless mind chose another path. Our local Lincoln Tech Institute was recruiting for auto mechanics, which interested me a great deal so off I went and soon became an auto mechanic for the next seven years.

Too many nights were spent awake and worrying about bills that I struggled to pay. As the TV played in the background, I started watching infomercials, and one in particular caught my attention. The 'No money down' commercial appealed to me so I figured, if they can make money in real estate then so can I!

In April of 2002, I attended my first real estate investment class. I was excited to buy, renovate, and flip homes but working two jobs got the best of me. In November of that same year, I was fired. I had never been fired from a job before in my life, but I wasn't too concerned about it because that's how mechanics take a vacation — and why our toolboxes have wheels!!

I consciously put my toolbox aside and devoted 50-60 hours weekly to my real estate business. It was a rough 90 days after that, and I wondered if I was making the right decision. I finally found my first deal and put it under contract. I sold my interest in this property for a fee and this is what we call 'wholesaling'. I made a lot of money in just three days and thus my new career was off to a start! So, I did it again and again and again and tripled my income in my first year! I never went back to working on cars — no surprise here.

I got my real estate license in the summer of 2003, the same year I began flipping houses. I enjoy it so much I continue to flip houses to this day. During the crash of 2008, my business plateaued, and I was forced to pivot to stay 'alive'. I opened my own brokerage and ran that successfully. Today, I am an associate broker and Operations Manager with EXIT Right Realty®. My main responsibilities are recruiting and retaining agents and building our brand.

Backing up a bit, my life was greatly affected when our family home went into foreclosure. I was eight years old when my father lost his job and could not sustain our family home. We moved to a small apartment in Jamaica, Queens, and I lost touch with my close friends. Fast forward, 17 years to age 25 when my sister and I were able to buy my family a house, and we moved back to our old neighborhood. Having a family home and then losing it sparked my desire never to let this happen again. To this day, I work with people facing foreclosure and help them keep their homes.

A CONNECTOR

Community comes first. People come first. I consider myself a connector at heart. This role charges my energy every day and allows me to form and grow my sphere of influence. I have resources, knowledge and information that is valuable to people, and I have no problem sharing it all. It simply makes me feel good to be the conduit that makes things happen!

I started working with Parkbench this year. I work with them because I believe in their system, and I value the Local Leader ® mentality. For instance, I get a kick out of it when someone says, "Everywhere we go..." I can't seem to venture too far without running into someone I know or hear a holler across the way, "Hey Anthony!"

I am working on building relationships with local businesspeople to the point where our rapport becomes our common ground. I envision walking into a restaurant and the owner steps in and gives me the best table! I dare to dream.

A GAME CHANGER

A particular story comes to mind that exemplifies what my business is all about. While I was in University I would walk to and from school passing a convenience store along the way. Not thinking much of it at the time, I later became the owner of that same commercial property.

I bought this property because its owners were facing foreclosure and in addition, their primary residence was attached as a guarantee, so they faced losing it as well. In addition, there was a lien on the building which made things even more difficult. They contacted me only five days before it was going into foreclosure. I was able to put the deal together, so they did not lose any money and most importantly they kept their home.

Having connections and helping people is my ultimate end game. Having lost my home and forced out as a young child, I know the hardships that come with leaving your friends and starting over.

HUMAN NATURE HAS ALWAYS FASCINATED ME

When I first started with Exit Realty® I became acutely aware of what personality types were and how they affected my day-to-day dealings with people. I was given the opportunity to take the DiSC® assessment, which is a questionnaire that analyzes one personality type. I discovered that I was a 'C' type. Some of my key attributes are detail-oriented, focused, strive for excellence, and conscientious.

I'm a 'dip my toes in first' kind of person who is initially cautious but once I feel comfortable, you will have my full attention. It has been said about me, "If you want to do something you will do it the best way you know how." Having said all this, I am deeply involved in relationship building both inside and outside of my business.

One of my challenges that I continue to work on is when it comes to people, I am an 'all-in guy' which can leave me vulnerable and sometimes leads to getting hurt. Not all relationships will be successful, and I sometimes have to remind myself that others may not reciprocate my thoughtfulness.

I continue to work on putting my emotions into place and manage them better. For example, I brought a friend into a real estate deal, and he ended up not paying me from his end of the transaction. I told him how I felt, and he chose not to make it right. I ended that relationship, but it didn't stop me from moving forward and making new relationships.

To do this, you have to love unapologetically. Most often when you are friends with someone, you know their friends and family too.

Cutting these ties leaves the door wide open for new love to come in. It's much like cutting the diseased part of a tree for the rest of it to flourish.

OUR '*EXIT*' STRATEGY

Everything that works, may not work for you. The number one thing that works all the time is consistency. This coupled with detailed analysis or testing will create a successful strategy. You can't know what you need to know unless you measure it. It goes back to the adage: 'Test, measure, decide.'

I take notes on everything I do. I try different messaging on different targets and then measure the response. In essence, I am learning the language to 'talk' to my future clients. I don't do anything randomly because that is a waste of time.

What works well at 'EXIT' is your sphere of influence. Relationship marketing is about reaching out to people who already know, like, and trust you. Working on a team is also fundamental as people want to follow leaders who know what they are doing. Our team has over 60 years combined experience and we use this to our advantage.

Leveraging our experience helps us build our teams across the board. We take pride in the training and mentorship programs we have designed. Each agent gets an opportunity to meet and spend time with the owners of EXIT Realty® which is a departure from most brokerages. The members of our leadership team make themselves available to help. I personally walk each representative step by step through our comprehensive training. You are not alone in this — we've got your back!

At EXIT we believe better is better . . . not more is better. We purposely keep our numbers down, so we do not dilute the quality of our people and their work. In essence, we are building our tribe with intention. New agents can become paralyzed and overwhelmed by the amount of learning that is required in this industry. So, grooming our team is vital to our existence.

As a fun analogy to emphasize quality and care, I believe one should be good at making two drinks and make them the best you can! I make the best Gin & Tonic and Old Fashioned because I carefully curate them with the best ingredients (Hendricks Gin with Fever Tree tonic and Woodford Reserve® Bourbon — in case you were wondering).

CREATING OUR TRIBE

We are ideally looking for the right fit when it comes to our team development. We can have full-timers, part-timers, but not some-timers. This business requires a minimum of 10 hours per week to gain momentum and earn a decent living.

The best agents are loyal, supportive, and willing to help others. We are willing to help work on deficiencies and use the DiSC® Method to help us determine what areas need improvement and what areas we can capitalize on. Our focus with a new agent isn't to sell a house right away, it is to ensure they have the proper tools in place to help them build their own successes.

The first step is to get someone in front of you or on a Zoom call and do a buyer presentation. I will help by being there by your side all the way. We record these sessions so you can pattern your own style and get comfortable with the systems. You express your value to your client up front, so they have full understanding of what's involved in the commissions payable.

THE EXIT FORMULA

In reality, most brokerages do not offer their agents anything close to what we do. EXIT is built on five pillars. The first pillar is training. Most offices offer training with either video or in person training. At EXIT we additionally offer mentorship and coaching. At the corporate, regional, broker, management, and peer levels we are here to give you information and help, just-in-time.

The second pillar is branding. Most brokers brand themselves. At EXIT, we believe clients buy from people, not companies.

Our third pillar is technology. Like my $1,000 cell phone, most of the tools, Realtors® tools have bells and whistles rarely used by them. Text my last name 'Beharry' to the five-digit phone number '85377' and hit send to see a sample our high tech and high touch tech.

Our fourth Pillar is our culture. We have a culture of fun and togetherness. We work together, much like a good family would. I am almost burned out from all the events and happy hours — almost. ☺

Finally, pillar five is the EXIT formula. The EXIT formula is unique in the industry in so far as we offer earnings above commissions alone. Anyone who joins our team will receive a 10% royalty for sponsoring and inviting others into our team which helps feed our culture. In addition, one's business is willable which offers a residual income for your heirs for their lifetime. So, if you want to hear more, tell your local EXIT broker Anthony Beharry sent you. ☺ It will be the best hour you ever spent.

GETTING OUT OF MY OWN WAY

If I had a talk with my younger self, I would offer myself some sage advice.

First, I would get out my own way and get away from my ego. I used to be so hard-headed, although my best friend, Ernie says I still am. I was hard on myself.

Second, I wouldn't be afraid to ask for help. I now realize it takes a village to create the business and systems I have now, but I could have done it quicker and easier if I had just reached out and asked for help.

Last, but not least, I feared obstacles that really weren't there. I have learned to manage mad, sad, and scared and put them into their boxes where they belong. I have now replaced these with peace, power, and joy and I am living my best life!

FINAL THOUGHTS

One of the most relevant books in my life is *The Magic of Thinking Big* by David Swartz. It's important to me because it gets me out of my comfort zone and challenges me to rise above my challenges.

• • •

I want to thank my blood family, my EXIT family, and my Parkbench family. As well as the family I choose my friends and neighbors.

Anthony Beharry

REACH OUT TO ANTHONY BEHARRY

abeharry@exitrightrealty.com
www.anthonybeharry.com
https://facebook.com/CapitolCityDCRealEstate
https://www.linkedin.com/in/dcmdrealestate
https://twitter.com/DC_MDRealEstate
https://www.instagram.com/anthonybeharry_realestate https://www.youtube.com/AnthonyBeharry

WHAT CLIENTS ARE SAYING ABOUT ANTHONY

"I have known Anthony Beharry for several years now. I have worked with him, and Anthony has always been a stand-up guy! Anthony is very passionate about helping and assisting others. He is very knowledgeable about the world of Real Estate on the Retail and Investment side...."

~TB, Washington DC

"OMG! Our experience with Anthony and EXIT Realty was awesome from beginning to end. Anthony and Ellen are full of knowledge and very professional. Anthony took the time to determine our needs and went above and beyond to meet every expectation...."

~MH, Waldorf, MD

"He is very professional, and he helped me a great deal with the process of selling my parent's home."

~YJ, Upper Marlboro, MD

ABOUT EXIT RIGHT REALTY

EXIT Right Realty has a philosophy of quality-client services. We demonstrate this through our regular training, coaching, and support. As part of the management staff here, we give this personal touch. It produces the most knowledgeable, well-equipped, and flexible agents that achieve EXIT's highest ethical standards. Striving for excellence will empower EXIT Right Realty, myself, and the Realtors® here; to become the most successful company in this region.

I have appeared on the Joe Madison and John Peterson show on WOL AM radio. Additionally, I have appeared on the Primetime News show with Peter Jennings. Most recently, I've interviewed on Great Day Washington. I am a Washington Real Estate Investing Association (REIA) member. I have taught members about foreclosures and general questions for three years. I love my work and passionately enjoy sharing my knowledge with clients and other estate agents. Using my proven system, I have successfully mentored hundreds of Realtors® and investors in all aspects of real estate.

CHAPTER 16

MEET ME IN MISSISSAUGA

" WHAT MANY PEOPLE DON'T REALIZE IS THAT THIS BUSINESS IS NOT ABOUT HOUSES, IT IS ABOUT PEOPLE, SO BUILDING RELATIONSHIPS IS THE KEY TO SUCCESS."

LAMBROS B. DEMOS
MISSISSAUGA, ON

GET TO KNOW LAMBROS B. DEMOS

Lambros Bryan Demos is a seasoned and award-winning Real Estate Broker who helps his clients navigate through the noise and frenzy of the current real estate market so they can win every time they buy or sell a home.

Lambros regularly creates relevant content for social media, and hosts live shows and seminars (both in-person and virtual) targeting investors, first-time home buyers, and downsizing seniors.

He is a top producer in his organization, consistently ranking among the top 10% in the country (out of 20,000+ agents).

Passionate about his community and giving back. Lambros is among the top donors of the Royal LePage Shelter Foundation, organizes an annual charity soccer tournament for ALS Canada and regularly spotlights and supports local businesses on social media.

For his expertise, Lambros has appeared on-air as a guest speaker on CHTO AM 1690 and CHIN FM 91.9 in Toronto, been interviewed on local television, quoted and interviewed in Authority Magazine, MSN.com, several podcasts, and been a repeat guest on Ticker | NEWS, a premier international news streaming network viewed over 2.2 million times per month.

MEET ME IN MISSISSAUGA

LAMBROS B. DEMOS

Is there anything more dramatic in sports than penalty kicks to decide a championship soccer match? This is how the 2013 North Mississauga U13 Boys House League Final ended, in my second year coaching the team. We had finished atop the standings - primarily due to some excellent goalkeeping by a young lad named Curtis - and we were now playing for the house league championship against the only team that beat us (twice, in fact) during the regular season. For some reason, they had our number but we now found ourselves tied after 90 minutes of regulation and 30 minutes of overtime. On to penalty kicks! In this best-of-5 contest, my team was up by a goal and our opponent was down to their last shot. They needed to score to stay alive. Curtis, however, had other ideas. He had played brilliantly the entire match and now it came down to one save. Just one more save and we will go home as champions. The enemy player lined up to take the kick. He strikes a beauty heading for the left corner but Curtis dives the correct way just in time to block the ball from going in the net! Game over. We win! My team and I race to the field, jumping for joy, and diving into the melee of players piling on top of Curtis. The parents on the sidelines cheered exuberantly. It had been an amazing season for this team, a dream year, and this victory helped deepen some already solid relationships between the players and me, as well as their parents. I coached six years for North Mississauga Soccer Club (NMSC), and even though I haven't coached since 2017, I am still getting referrals and repeat business from these families to this day, from the relationships that were made during that time.

Don't get me wrong, I am not saying you have to coach a winning soccer team to get real estate referrals but it sure was fun! When I started with NMSC, I was thinking how could I get involved in the community? How could I build relationships with people so they would know me, like me, and trust me enough to work with me as their realtor? Let me start further back, however. Let's go back to the early 90s when I first fell in love with Mississauga.

I was living in Toronto at the time and used to come to Mississauga – a west end suburb of Toronto but also an important industrial centre in its own right - to visit a friend who lived on Elizabeth Street in Port Credit, the south end of the city by Lake Ontario. We would walk down to Lakeshore Blvd, visit the various pubs and just enjoy the vibe. That vibrancy still exists today, with so much diversity and energy, and gorgeous scenery, not just in Port Credit but all around the city. Mississauga is actually made up of several distinct small villages, each having its own look and feel, and that's what makes it special

Going even further back, to the early 1970s, nine unique villages (Clarkson, Cooksville, Dixie, Erindale, Lakeview, Lorne Park, Port Credit, Sheridan, and Summerville) amalgamated into Mississauga. Today, that number has grown to 24 communities, and each neighbourhood still carries its own unique characteristics: from picturesque Port Credit to bustling Hurontario; from the bungalows of Applewood (an actual apple orchard up until the early 20th century) to the high rise condos of City Centre; and from the industrial Northeast to the small town flair of Streetsville.

The late 1990s to early 2000s brought me to Mississauga on a regular basis and this is also when I first started coaching soccer. This time it was my little sister's rep soccer team (North York Cosmos based in Toronto's north end) and we would take on local clubs in Mississauga like Dixie, Erin Mills, and the aforementioned NMSC. I absolutely loved the ambience here as well as the parks where the teams would play. They were always pristine and welcoming. One could tell that the community cared about the sport and that meant a lot to me. Since the team I was coaching was a competitive rep team, I was allowed to recruit players from outside of North York and it so happened that a number of these recruited players lived in Mississauga, so on occasion, I would drive them home from games, tournaments, or practices. This allowed me to conveniently explore the various neighbourhoods. I admired the large lots and variety of homes, particularly in the south end, such as Mineola, Lakeview, Lorne Park, and Clarkson.

At that time, I was working as a registered massage therapist (RMT) but had an affinity for real estate. I was familiar with real estate because my mother was in the business during the late 80s and early 90s. I would watch how she operated, negotiated, and hustled. She would also bring me with her occasionally to check out houses to potentially buy as investment properties. I would then help her with renovations, property management, tenant management, etc.

In 2011, I decided to transition into real estate myself and studied to get my license. Mississauga was a natural destination for my new career choice, not only due to my affinity for the place but also because this area has always been a high demand area for real estate. Being so close to Toronto, many people find it to be a more enjoyable and cheaper option to live in rather than in the big city, so it is and always has been a great spot for commuters. It also attracts many newcomers to Canada with the proximity to Pearson International Airport, the sheer amount of high-rise residential buildings, predominantly in the central core, as well as an abundance of employment opportunities, especially in the aforementioned northeast part of the city, which has numerous factories. It is also only about an hour's drive to the popular tourist destination of Niagara Falls.

Before even finishing my real estate courses, I was invited to interview at my current brokerage. This was my one and only job interview. Walking into the office for the first time, I was amazed at the modern look and friendly atmosphere. I knew instantly that I wanted to work here. As I was waiting to be interviewed, I saw a framed photo of the brokerage's core values:

- Integrity
- Professionalism
- Competence
- Respect for individuals
- Productivity
- Financial responsibility

These values resonated with me. Since I share these same values, there was now no doubt in my mind that this was the place where I wanted to hang my hat. My interview with the brokerage owner went splendidly and I was offered a job before even completing my final licensing course.

Upon getting my license, I discovered quickly how competitive this business is. Call it naivety but I assumed because I had great relationships with my previous clients in massage therapy — some of them were completely devoted to me — I thought they would naturally hire me if and when they needed real estate services. Boy, was I wrong! My first mistake was not taking into consideration that these people already had relationships with real estate agents, so it is hard to challenge that, especially as a fresh, new agent. Secondly, they loved me as their RMT, so they couldn't see me (or maybe couldn't accept me) as anything else. Not everyone thought this way, however, as a few massage clients did actually hire me to buy and/or sell a home.

At this point, I realized I had to start from scratch and build new relationships. What made my RMT practice so successful was these relationships and the repeat and referral business that came from them. Real estate is the same way. What many people don't realize is that this business is not about houses, it is about people, so building relationships is the key to success.

I wanted to be known as a local leader, and someone who the community looked up to and trusted but how do I get the ball rolling? Then it hit me like a soccer ball to the face! I would go back to what I loved doing — coaching — so I signed on with NMSC as a coach and sponsor. I thought this would be a great way to meet people and get involved in the community! This time I scored because I was able to build many great relationships through my involvement with NMSC. I coached for six years but still remain in contact today with several people I met through the club, like Curtis and his family.

Giving back as a community volunteer and club sponsor was one way of becoming a local leader. I wasn't just a name and logo on a soccer jersey, I was a real person who people got to know. I made sure to speak to all the parents, whether on the sidelines of a game, or as they picked up and dropped off their kids from practice. I also made myself available by phone and email whenever a mom or dad wanted to talk about their child's progress. At the end of each soccer season, I would organize a friendly parents vs. players match and that was always a blast! I would then treat the players to a meal at one of the local restaurants — and, of course, invite the parents, and this would give me an opportunity to get to know them even better. This also supported local business so it was a win-win-win all the way around.

Speaking of local leaders, I think my values and my brokerage's values (as listed above) fall in line with what a local leader should be.

In 2018, my business picked up significantly so I could not commit to coaching soccer anymore. Evenings and weekends are prime time for realtors, so I didn't want to be "that coach" in title only — who did not show up consistently and left the bulk of the games and practices to his assistant(s). That would lead people to question my commitment and integrity. Instead of coaching, I found other ways to give back such as organizing charity soccer tournaments, client appreciation parties at local businesses, etc.

When the pandemic reared its ugly head, Ontario was hit pretty hard with lockdowns. This was a death sentence for many small businesses across the province and Mississauga was no exception. I thought about how I could help local business owners and came up with a new community brand on social media called "Meet Me in Mississauga". The purpose was to spotlight and support local businesses, as well as provide people with weekly information about the best places to eat, shop, volunteer, and have fun — which had become slim pickings during the lockdowns! Earlier this year, the lockdowns were lifted once and for all (hopefully), everything opened up, and people resumed a somewhat normal routine. The original intent for "Meet Me is Mississauga" did not seem as relevant anymore so I was ready to shut it down but then I discovered Parkbench and thought this could 10x my mission! I am now in the process of rebranding "Meet Me in Mississauga" with an amazing new website featuring video interviews with local business owners (instead of just picture posts), local listings, and much more! This came about at the perfect time and fit in nicely with my values and goals.

The other reason why I like Parkbench is because it allows me to go the extra mile. Coincidentally, "Going the extra mile" is my motto but it's more than just a tagline. It is how I run my business. In fact, it's the only way I know *how* to do business. I don't believe in short cuts, I believe in providing a great experience. I don't want my clients to just be happy, I want to knock their socks off with my service so they can become advocates for me. As bestselling author and high-performance coach, Randy Garn, once told a group of us, "If they like you, they will listen to you. If they trust you, they will buy from you but give them a great experience and they will never ever leave you." Parkbench allows me to provide a great experience to my community and to my clients.

Lambros Demos

REACH OUT TO LAMBROS B. DEMOS

Lambros B. Demos, SRES
Broker
Royal LePage Realty Plus
416-520-0222

WHAT CLIENTS ARE SAYING ABOUT LAMBROS

> *"We highly recommend Lambros. He was able to help educate us throughout the entire process from listing our home to helping us find our dream home without us having to compromise our wants and needs. Lambros is very professional and takes the extra steps to ensure you are protected with the biggest investment of your life, his honesty is very refreshing in today's world."*

~ Heather & Tony N.

"Lambros came highly recommended from family friends for his professionalism and honesty. Lambros helped us buy the home of our dreams and sell our home under challenging circumstances. The buying process was stressful and competitive, but Lambros helped us stay grounded, calm, and stand out among other buyers. Lambros also did the same while selling our home with the added challenge of a stay-at-home order. Within two weeks we had bought a house and sold our home and, while anxiety inducing, was as smooth as can be with Lambros's guidance and calm demeanor. He knows what he is doing and is so great at his job. We would recommend him to anyone!"

~Rick & Roberta P.

"After listening to testimonials and seeing the results from friends and neighbors we asked Lambros to sell our home. This guy was amazing! Communication was key. He heard us when we were describing our needs and goals. He was hands on and assisted us with supplies to pack and declutter. Lambros then arranged a home inspection to list repairs required and supply a Certified Resale Home Warranty. He then arranged a stager to suggest improvements that would maximize the value in our house. With a little effort we listed our home. Six days later we had over 60 viewings, resulting in multiple offers and selling over asking price. I would highly recommend Lambros to sell your home and like us, help fulfill your retirement dreams."

~ Dan & Sue C.

CHAPTER 17

FROM FAILURE TO FIRST

"My effort is designed to avoid distractions and not get trapped by negativity. Persistence and consistency can almost always erase these challenges. These are key factors to my business accomplishments. Ultimately, the goal is to have my clients realize their dreams too!"

Ces Guerra
Houston, TX

GET TO KNOW CES GUERRA

Ces was born and raised in New Orleans, LA. He is the eldest son of Latin American immigrants. During his high school years he was active in the YMCA of New Orleans, at that time the Y was the home of some of the finest athletes in various Olympic sports, ... he was NOT one of them.

After High School, he had a failed attempt at university life in the Fall of 1976 ... chemistry was the hurdle. During the Christmas break he enlisted in the U.S. Army and began his service in March of 1977. During Boot Camp, he was recruited to and joined the 82nd Airborne Division and served his four years of active duty in the 307th medical battalion at Ft Bragg, NC.

Honorably discharged in 1981, he gave the university life another shot and enrolled at LSU in Baton Rouge. Why chemistry was part of the Computer Science curriculum, he still doesn't know, but once again it was the challenge that altered his course. He graduated in December of 1984 with a Bachelor of Arts degree in Geography and began wandering the Earth!

His career took him from nonprofit work to corporate insurance claims, back to non-profit work and then to consumer and pharmaceutical sales for about 20 years. During his corporate sales career, he enrolled in the Houston Baptist Executive MBA program, graduating in 1994. He published his first book, Pill Pushers in 2007 and the hope is that one day someone will see the content as a potential big screen movie! His 2nd book, Gumbo for the Tiger Soul was published in 2014, and will NOT become a movie!

After departing the pharmaceutical industry, Ces continued his pursuit of success discovering a knack for residential real estate. Thankfully, chemistry is not involved in the real estate business!! Licensed in 2013 he has been a Top Producer the last 7 consecutive years and recognized as the Top Team in the River Oaks office of Better Homes & Gardens - Gary Greene for the past 2 consecutive years!

He is married to Laura Hawkins of New Orleans. Their adventures together have taken them from the summit of Mt. Kilimanjaro to the

Base Camp of Mt Everest and from the Andes to the Alps! While they do enjoy sailing on the water, they also enjoy diving below the surface with over 150 SCUBA dives!

FROM FAILURE TO FIRST

CES GUERRA

LEADERSHIP

A pivotal moment in my leadership journey happened as far back as All Saints Day in New Orleans in 1972. It was as if it happened yesterday as I remember the lessons I learned so clearly. I got into a fight with one of the boys I was hanging with and got a little roughed up — a black eye to be exact.

My mom was a strong woman who ruled with an iron fist, due in part to the fact that my dad was in the merchant marines and was away most of the time. She knew just what to do with me and my black eye. We went directly to the local YMCA where she enrolled me into a Judo class. I think she wanted me to be able to defend myself, as it were!

The next year I got involved with the Junior Leadership program at the 'Y' where I became a daytime camp counselor for the summer. I was an introvert by nature, and I felt out of place most of the time. Little did I know at the time that this experience would change my life forever. My road towards becoming a leader was being paved.

I have taken on many leadership roles over the years including during my time in my Army 82nd Airborne as a squad leader, as president of the Houston LSU Alumni Association, many roles during my time at college, and as a district manager at a large pharmaceutical company.

My love for volunteering and taking on leadership roles continues into my current life as I work with our local Christian Community Services Center teaching resume building and interview skills workshops.

WE CAN'T CONTROL THE WINDS BUT WE CAN ADJUST THE SAILS

My message of inspiration and encouragement has always been at the core of everything I do. I'm often asked to give speeches at local business clubs, non-profit groups and schools so I created a speech that acts as my boilerplate for these events. It is entitled *From Failure to First; My story of failures, struggles, lessons learned, and the pursuit of success.*

I've had my share of failures as a young man and growing up a Latin-American boy with English as my second language was only one of the challenges I faced. My parents were first-generation immigrants and they struggled to meet the daily demands of raising a young family in their new country. In addition, I struggled with fitting in and was often in 'trouble' because I didn't understand the rules and language.

Fast forward a bit, I attended the YMCA Blue Ridge Assembly Leadership Program where I learned how to teach. It was deeply entrenched in tradition, values, and faith and I was blessed with learning the process of becoming a coach and mentor for young kids. This gave me the foundation I needed to start my journey into leadership.

Another challenging time was my first experience with college. I nearly flunked out in my first year. I can still hear my mom saying, *"We are not paying for this."* In her next breath, *"Guess who's been calling — the Army recruiter."* As a good son, I went off to meet the recruiter.

The G.I. Bill was a government program that offered veterans benefits after their service. They offered to help pay for my college tuition if I enlisted before December 31, 1976. As you can guess, I signed on the dotted line. I served my tour of duty, received my honorable discharge on February 28, 1981, and enrolled at LSU in the fall of 1981.

As a Platoon Leader I was assigned to the 82nd- Airborne Division 307th Medical Battalion. As a paratrooper I was the first line of defense, and the training was quite rigorous. This was a very prestigious unit. I learned a great deal while enlisted and feel very proud of serving our country. Lessons were learned such as discipline and determination and of course, a famous quote: "Fatigue makes cowards of us all."

Despite the ups and downs of my young life, I learned to adjust to my circumstances and take on my next challenge with resiliency.

PERSISTENCE AND CONSISTENCY

In my pursuit of success, my eternal optimism keeps me moving forward. As the saying goes, *A journey of a thousand miles begins with a single step.* Sticking to a plan and adjusting accordingly helps mitigate problems that may present themselves daily. The real estate industry is no exception to the rule when it comes to constant change.

Today, I am at the top of my game and my career is truly a dream come true. I don't get distracted by low inventory, high interest rates, or a volatile market. My effort is designed to avoid distractions and not get trapped by negativity. Persistence and consistency can almost always erase these challenges. These are key factors to my business accomplishments. Ultimately, the goal is to have my clients realize their dreams too!

FUN FACTS ABOUT TANGLEWOOD, HOUSTON

As a resident since 1990, I describe Houston as the 'smallest-large' city in the world. Houston is the fourth largest city in America and yet, it has that small town feel. It is dotted with countless, unique little neighborhoods that have their own personalities.

Since 2006, I have called the Tanglewood neighborhood my home. I love the fact I can walk in any direction and get to my destination within minutes. Tanglewood Boulevard is lined with live oak trees that provide much-needed shade during the hot summer months. Many of the old and new houses are built from English-style brick or Mediterranean-style stucco which also help ward off the heat!

Tanglewood and Broad Oaks are near the geographic center of Houston. They are near some of the hotspots such as The Uptown Park, The Energy Corridor, The Galleria, and are equal distance to both major airports. As the saying in real estate goes, "Location, location, location!" Tanglewood's location provides great access to many of the fun things to do such as Astros baseball at Minute Maid Park, the Houston Livestock Show & Rodeo at NRG Stadium, the Houston Zoo at Hermann Park, and the Toyota Center for concerts and the Rockets!

BEYOND THE FOUR WALLS

My mom wanted me to be a social worker because she believed that serving one's fellow man was one of the highest honors. However, my path took a slightly different direction. After I left the pharmaceutical industry, I wanted to do something on my own, something that I could build on my own by leveraging my talents and the skills I had gained over the years.

I struck out on my own when I obtained my health and life insurance license. After several years of selling insurance, I obtained my real estate license in 2012 because I had an interest in it and knew Houston like the back of my hand.

Helping people find homes and helping local business owners build their clientele is what gets me up and running early every morning. My family values have shaped the way I do business in that I support locals when I can, and develop relationships with local businesses and influencers on a daily basis. Service to my community is my higher calling.

Equally important as finding my clients the best home possible is offering them the best neighborhood. I go beyond the four walls of a house by understanding the landscape of the communities in which that property is located. For instance, I have become the source of information for my clients and associates. Whether they're asking me about the commute, restaurants, schools, or the crime rates, I know exactly where to help them find the information. These things may seem insignificant on the surface, but to someone who is unfamiliar with the city or neighborhood this information is gold!

A BETTER BROKER

Not every brokerage is right for every agent, otherwise we would all be working for the same company. When I started out in real estate, I worked at a small brokerage that offered little in the way of support. I didn't know what I didn't know, so I floundered for some time trying to make sense of the business. I shared my struggles with a friend who worked with Better Homes and Gardens — Gary Greene — and he introduced me to his broker. Going in, I vowed to do my due diligence and not sign anything. Well, I signed everything THAT afternoon. Every piece of paperwork handed to me was executed that day!

I now spend my days mapping out my calendar, as time management is vital. I try to create daily improvements and am open to learning new and better ways of doing things. But I mostly like to have FUN! Without fun, I don't think I would do well in this business. Although conservative on the outside, I am pure Mardi Gras on the inside!

My team enjoys regular events like Top Golf outings and lunches where we can just be ourselves and enjoy our successes. Personally, I love to hike, swim, and above all else, travel wherever the wind takes us. I have visited numerous places, including 48 of the 50 states in America. My love of hiking has taken me to base-camp on Everest to the top of Mt. Kilimanjaro.

I am a fortunate man.

WHAT'S UNDER THE HOOD?

If I can offer any advice to someone considering real estate as a business:

- Do your due diligence when choosing a broker to work with.

- Keep an open mind because, particularly in your first year, people will come and go at a rate that will make your eyes cross; your mindset needs to remain positive.
- Get in-depth training. Do the work upfront that is necessary to move your business forward.
- Create a strong sphere of influence.
- Keep learning. Take classes, attend conferences, and read books!
- Don't deviate from your plan, if possible. I realize life can throw you curveballs and things can be out of your control, however, get back to your plan as soon as possible. Your business depends on it.

Throughout the course of my career, I have learned I can't do everything myself. I set my ego and pride aside and collaborate with mentors and working partners whenever possible. I put my trust in a mentor to help advise and guide me. I've also organized working partners who are in the "same boat" as I am and have formed "Mastermind" groups. Some might say it's the blind leading the blind, but I choose to look at it as an accountability group where we are safe to say we don't know or have all the answers.

TOOLS IN MY TOOLBOX

Over the years, I have tried and tested various software programs, lead generation techniques, marketing strategies, etc. I certainly believe anything will work if you work it! However, I do have my favorites that continue to work for me:

- Zillow can work, but don't spend too much time and money on this if you are not getting results.
- Invest time and money on a local level.
- Keep your CRM organized and your calendar up to date.
- KV Core, a tech company that provides agents with a huge, all-encompassing platform , offers DocuSign services, marketing tools, CRM, digital cards, and much more.

- Develop a good website that integrates with your social media, calendar, blogs, CRM, email capture, etc.

WRAPPING IT UP

Since my entry into the real estate business in 2008, I have been blessed with good fortune and great people around me. Keeping things in perspective has always served me well.

Perhaps you are trying to build a team, but people keep leaving — do it anyway. Perhaps you fell short of your goal last year. Redesign it and do it anyway. Regardless of what obstacles you may encounter in your personal or business life, face them head-on and get in front of them.

I want to take this opportunity to thank the wonderful people at Parkbench for supporting me and offering me more than I ever expected. This platform has helped elevate my business and I foresee a great deal of future success coming from this partnership.

There are many people to thank, and I can't thank them all. However, I'd like to thank Phil Leatherman, my first sales manager with Clairol back in 1990. I'd also like to thank Greg Fontenot, who demonstrated tough leadership and helped me develop my listening skills, which have helped me with every single client today! Finally, I'd like to thank JJ Molaison, my current broker manager, who changed my life. Not because of what she made me do, but because of the guidance and the illumination of options that helped me navigate the early years of my real estate career! There are countless others including my wife, Laura, my clients, and my teammates — past and present! It's the team that keeps me going and keeps the journey fun!

Ces Guerra

REACH OUT TO CES GUERRA

The Guerra Group
Better Home and Gardens RE Gary Greene-Tanglewood
713-298-6070
https://www.instagram.com/theguerragroup
https://www.facebook.com/theguerragroup
https://www.linkedin.com/in/cesguerra

WHAT CLIENTS ARE SAYING ABOUT CES

> *"Ces is awesome! Very professional and walked me through every detail! I would highly recommend him to anyone! He always gave me options and information that I found very helpful. I will definitely use him again when I decide to look for a new place."*

~Bobby Ware ***** *Five* Star *Rating*

> *"Ces and his team are professional and walk you through everything from start to finish. Ces will be selling my old home and I trust his judgment. I have enjoyed working with Ces and his team."*

~Nickie Landry ***** Five Star Rating

> *"Ces the agent was the main reason that I chose the brokerage (and I am glad I did). I did not know the Gary Greene Inner Loop before that. Ces was amaz-*

ingly professional, knowledgeable, approachable, polite and friendly. And it was a great experience to work with him. He surely made the journey of purchasing the house smooth and pleasant. Great experience, and I would recommend anyone to Ces Guerra and Gary Greene Inner Loop office."

~Gilbert Mishly ***** Five Star Rating

CHAPTER 18

LETTING MY LIGHT SHINE

" Whatever their budget, everyone deserves a caring, conscientious guide in the home buying or selling process. It's not simple and I love being able to explain and coach. It's like being a guide through an unknown land. I like being able to point out where the quicksand and the alligators are."

Glenda Koernig
Mesa, AZ

GET TO KNOW GLENDA KOERNIG

A guide. A coach. A problem solver. Whether it's figuring out which home is the best, helping to find financing solutions, getting an offer accepted in today's competitive market, negotiating prices, or handling the details of closing, buyers soon discover Glenda is a reliable resource. Sellers appreciate her market savvy, attention to detail, and quiet competence. She believes everyone deserves a GREAT home buying or selling experience and devotes herself to that end.

People who want to buy or sell a home, and win at the game, use Glenda because she outmaneuvers the competition. She helps her clients navigate the process, get the deal done, and have peace of mind. Bottom line, she is the trusted adviser of their dreams.

Since 1996 Glenda has been helping buyers and sellers navigate successfully through the maze of acquiring or selling a home. She's a great listener and cares about you! She is solution oriented and a fantastic sounding board. She's compassionate, yet analytical. She is nurturing, yet practical.

Glenda grew up on a small farm in South Carolina and received a BA in English from Furman University where she was a James B. Duke scholar. She was an army wife for 10 years and spent three years in Germany. Then, as a single mom, she helped her four children grow up to be happy, successful adults.

Glenda has lived in NC, CA, and the Pacific NW, but Arizona has become home. She is happily married to novelist and former Billings, MT evening news anchor, Gus Koernig, and lives in the Riverview area of Mesa, AZ.

LETTING MY LIGHT SHINE

GLENDA KOERNIG

West Mesa, where I live, is the oldest part of Mesa, AZ. It all but touches Phoenix and was settled in 1877 by Mormon pioneers. When I first moved here, I thought of it as Phoenix's smaller, country cousin. It's the size of Atlanta, GA — not so small and not so country. It is home to Apple, Google, Meta, and some of the fasting growing residential areas in the country. During the housing boom of 2000-2008, many of the residents of West Mesa bought bigger and better to the east. Left behind were those who could not afford to move. Hard working Hispanics, looking to become homeowners, filled in the gaps along with my new husband, Gus and I in 2012. We were Mormons ourselves, had raised large families, didn't have a lot of resources, but were also determined to become homeowners again ourselves.

Don't get me wrong. There were also many who liked where they were living and didn't want to move. Another draw to the area is its proximity to Tempe, Chandler, and Scottsdale. Not everyone was willing to drive the extra 30 to 45 minutes to the newer parts of town. Others preferred the diversity over the sameness of East Mesa.

Even though some people thought of this as the slums, rehabbing had already started to happen in the area when I chose 85201, my home address, as my Zillow zip code in 2013 when I started advertising as a Premier Agent. Renovations really took off when the Chicago Cubs began building Sloan Park, which opened in 2014. Spring training is a big deal here, a really big deal.

I could have chosen areas with pricier homes with the bigger commissions, but I made the decision to be local. The leads I got through Zillow, however, ended up taking me from one end of Maricopa County to the other. I went wherever I needed to go to match my buyers with properties that matched their needs.

My biggest opportunity came when I was chosen to represent Envision Capital Management on the Main Street Station townhome project at 1406 W Main in Mesa, based on my understanding of values and expertise in 85201 zip code. It turned out to be a seven-year project, 2015-2022. This experience really fine-tuned my skills of working with a builder, appraisals, marketing, financing, and seller representation. Also, I loved the diversity of the buyers and the challenge of working with many different cultures. I learned how creative and adaptive I could be.

Representing the seller on the 42 townhomes at Main Street Station showcased my ability to adapt to a client's needs. The project was privately funded and well suited to a re-development area. The pace of sales in its first years was less important than getting the price we wanted for these units, which exceeded the quality and value of other homes in the area. Even though the third and final phase was delayed by the pandemic, we were able to bring it to market amid supply and labor shortages — when housing demand was at its highest — and sold it out quickly. Mike Druckman, my contact at Envision Capital, said I was a dream to work with. As always, I put my client's needs and wishes first, even when they went against conventional wisdom.

Fortunately for me, since I was the listing agent instead of an employee of the developer, I could represent other clients at the same time. In 2019, I earned my Accredited Buyer Representative (ABR), Seller Representative Specialist (SRS), and Real Estate Negotiation Expert (RENE) which put me into their referral network. ABR is a designation issued by the Real Estate Buyer's Agent Council and the National Association of REALTORS® (NAR). SRS and RENE are both certifications of the Real Estate Business Institute, and affiliates of

NAR. I felt these credentials would show my commitment to excellence and add value to the services I could offer as a real estate agent. They also helped build my business.

I got into real estate because having a home matters to me. What doesn't matter is what you can afford. Whatever their budget, everyone deserves a caring, conscientious guide in the home buying or selling process. It's not simple and I love being able to explain and coach. It's like being a guide through an unknown land. I like being able to point out where the quicksand and the alligators are.

A person buys or sells a home both with their heart and their mind. I like being able to tune in to both aspects and help each client be at peace at the end of the process; confident they have made the best decision possible.

Relationship and referral based is the only way to go, whenever possible. One of the reasons I stopped being a Zillow Premier Agent was because it was so transactional. The average conversation rate for leads is 6%. That means, as an agent, you are spending a lot of time with people who do not wish to engage with you. I don't mind if you change your mind or if you don't want to do business with me. But I much prefer mutual respect and cordiality.

To me, a Local Leader is someone who actively takes ownership of the impact possible in a community; someone who consciously looks for ways to improve it or be positive about it or support and celebrate it. I am community focused because that is an important aspect of being a homeowner. We don't live on an island. The spirit each individual homeowner brings to the community has an impact. I make it a point to be the best neighbor I can be. Also, I go to church in my neighborhood and give service there.

I feel and sense deeply the need for home as a place of safety, security, refuge, and a center for creativity. Since I am committed to cultivating myself as the highest expression of myself, I know I need a context for this creation.

I'm a lot like West Mesa. I could be bitter and resentful because of some of the disappointments in my life, but I have learned to choose gratitude. I want to embody *joie de vivre,* even though I "live in an older neighborhood" speaking figuratively about this stage of my life. I want to build vibrancy in myself and my community. I celebrate diversity. I embrace my own creativity and am breaking through old conditionings that had too often shut me down. I am opening my heart to radical self-love/compassion and turning that outward to my community. I am decluttering inwardly and outwardly. I am harvesting from my life experiences. I champion recycling and composting. It is fitting that I find myself, my home, my neighbors, and my community, in an area of revitalization.

I know the world is not a place where everyone has access to what they need to develop their potential and give their gifts to the world, but I do what I can to give what I can and support others whenever I can.

I serve from my heart and soul. I intend to make an even greater difference in my life and the lives of others. The world has enough critics. It needs more champions, more caring. I am learning to let my heart off the leash.

I went a lot of years without a home. I had a place to stay, but I was not a homeowner. As a military wife, I moved around a lot. After 10 years and four children I wanted the bathroom to be in the same place when I got up in the middle of the night. Then there were some rocky years after my divorce when I was barely getting by. I hungered for a place of my own. That feeling is one of the things I bring to the process. And I know the feeling of disruption that comes with moving.

My empathy for the discomfort of change and dealing with unknowns is one of my strengths.

Also, I understand the feeling of wanting to get it right while dealing with multiple, and sometimes conflicting, needs and wants. Once my four children were in four different schools and each needed something. I only had my lunch hour and had to decide which need was most life threatening. I've been told I have a knack for helping others cut through the noise, to help them see what matters most when they are trying to decide, settle on a strategy, or get clarity. My life helped me do that for myself and I really like helping others do the same.

When Warren Buffet was asked for an investment recommendation in early 2022, he said invest in yourself. I've done that. I upgraded my computer equipment and printer and, more importantly, I've invested in coaches and programs to help me with my mindset.

When I started working in real estate, I was a single mom with children still at home. I remember thinking I needed to focus on the money to make the income I needed. Somehow, I noticed or realized that when I focused on the people instead of the money, my business thrived. It was a mindset change.

I've also struggled with visibility. Where I grew up, how much money you had, and your social standing played a big part in how you were valued and treated. I was the daughter of a small farmer who also worked in the cotton mills. My mother never wrote a check or learned to drive a car. We lived 15 miles out of the wrong side of town and there was no money or transportation for me to participate in after school activities. I couldn't be in the band or anything like that. I was so thrilled when I was asked to be the co-editor of my junior high yearbook. And so broken hearted when my father said no. Even though I got good grades and eventually a scholarship to the finest university in the state, it took me a long time to appreciate my worth. That early isolation took its toll on me.

It took me a while to learn to trust my heart; to trust my ability to take on challenges and solve puzzles, even very complex problems; to realize I had the ability to understand the legal issues and take a stand where necessary. I have found a willingness to give, and adjust to reach agreements and resolutions, are important tools in my toolbox.

Once a former colleague, who I trusted, cut me out while closing on a deal I had put together for the sale of his home. It was a very challenging, time-consuming transaction and he paid me almost nothing. This was at a time when I was strapped financially. It made me want to get out of real estate. Later, I realized he just didn't have the money to pay me, and I was able to forgive him. But it took a while.

Another time I helped one of my buyers escape the pitfalls of her previous predatory agent. He had her sign a Buyer Broker agreement without her knowledge or consent and had been trying to push her into a purchase she didn't want. After we closed on a condo of her choice, that agent had an attorney send her a letter demanding that she pay him a commission as well, based on the agreement she didn't know she had signed. I got the feeling it was a form letter that had been used many times. Ignoring the demand letter would have resulted in a judgement against her for $4,000+. After examining all the articles of the Realtor Code of Ethics and the requirements of the Arizona Association of Realtors®, I helped her write a response accompanied by prefilled proper forms in readiness to file a complaint. They backed down and released her from that obligation if she would sign an agreement not to name them publicly going forward. I felt really good about that. Of course, this was all done at no additional charge to her.

Right at the start of the pandemic, a buyer's loan failed to fund on the scheduled day of closing. Although she was able to quickly switch over to a VA loan through her father, since he would be living with her, the seller, who I represented, totally freaked out. It was a sure thing, but he wouldn't sign the addendum to the contract allowing this to happen. As I continued to communicate with him, I finally began to understand his emotions. The solution — I withdrew a sum of my money in cash for him to hold until it closed. I knew it would close and I knew he could be trusted to return the cash to me at closing. He signed the addendum, and all was well.

On another occasion, my friend's sister was living in a house she owned jointly with their mother. Their mom died in 2009, but the estate never went through probate. This sister had another family member and his girlfriend living in the house. She was being bullied and was ready to be welcomed into her married daughter's home in another state. The house was very cluttered and in disrepair. I used my connections to find a reputable probate attorney to get the ball rolling and put up the money for the deposit, knowing I would get it back at closing. I got multiple offers on her house by using a professional photographer to capture comprehensive shots of the home to post on a website I created. I knew just what a rehabber would need to know, to compel them to buy the house. We quickly got it under contract for a good price, with minimal drama. I got the other brothers and sisters added to the contract so the proceeds could be easily distributed between them at closing. The saving grace was the division of funds was undisputed. The rehabber who purchased it praised my website and said he had never had a deal like this go so smoothly.

What has worked for me is recognizing, owning, and using my unique gifts, talents, and abilities. I have confidence now. I know I have what it takes to get the job done, no matter what. At last, I can give up thinking I should be more like everybody else.

My clients love working with me because they know they are in good hands. I am patient with their process and make sure they always have the information they need to feel good about their decisions as they move forward. I don't like to be pushed or pressured. No one else likes it either.

A few years ago, I realized the only thing holding me back was me. I knew I had to change my energy. I was taking good care of my clients, but I wasn't doing a very good job of taking care of me. A pattern of self-neglect can be prevalent in the world we live in, but it isn't sustainable. I learned the key to changing my energy toward others was the change I was making toward myself. Remember that counsel to love others as you love yourself? You can imagine what loving myself better and more completely did for my relationship with others!

The Feminine Power programs by Claire Zammit have been very instrumental in helping me come out of my shell and feel confident in expressing my authenticity, liking who I am, and getting comfortable with my place in the world. I had tried a lot of other things, but this really worked for me. This system helped me feel safer in showing and expressing my brilliance.

I had a small brokerage of my own in NC, but I won't do that again. I want to stay square with the state, but I don't want to deal with it personally. With state audits it's not if, it's when. I represented a retired homebuilder in Portland, OR in an IRS audit of a complex financial year. I also updated and audited the files of the brokerage where I worked in Oregon. So, I know I can do it, I just prefer not to. Also, I make sure I have a broker who is extremely knowledgeable about the rules and regulations of real estate. There are any number of ways things can go wrong. Whenever anything comes into dispute, I want to know exactly where to make a stand.

One final observation — if you want to have a business built on integrity (and I recommend you do), limit your contact and exposure to those without it as much as possible. There are wolves in sheep's clothing out there, but they eventually show their true colors. Then you know what to do, move away as quickly and as far as you can.

I'm grateful to Parkbench. It is an excellent, pre-built platform that I intend to use to give value to my community. It is an incentive to grow myself in the direction I want to grow. I will interview various service providers, especially small businesses, and entrepreneurs. The interviews and accompanying free website I can provide them will help local providers build their businesses. Homeowners want to know who they can turn to for trustworthy and competent care. I have already been providing this kind of information, upon request, for past clients and friends, so this will build upon what I am already doing.

I'm so excited about building my proficiency in photography and videography as I promote my community through Parkbench. I must admit, I'm still a little shy about setting up the interviews and following through on the contacts I am making. Once I get into it more, I know I will love it! I'm excited about Parkbench as a tool to help make a difference in my life and to help others in my community. I have to give a shout out to the wonderful support team at Parkbench. They are an integral part of my success story!

Glenda Koernig

REACH OUT TO GLENDA KOERNIG

Glenda Koernig ABR, SRS, RENE
Real Estate Agent / Kenneth James Realty
480-694-0890
7720 N Dobson Rd, Scottsdale AZ 85256
AZpropertiesByGlenda@gmail.com

WHAT CLIENTS ARE SAYING ABOUT GLENDA

"Glenda will work to get the job done for you rain or shine without the demeanor of a slimy salesperson. She means what she says and does what she promises. Working with Glenda from out of state was a joy for my wife and me. In-state folks are guaranteed top notch service as well. Glenda is very responsive via phone, text, AND email. She knows buyers and sellers need this level of attention. Glenda can work with first-time buyers as well as seasoned investors. She knows how to read clients and respond to their needs appropriately. Glenda is on-time and doesn't get lost trying to find properties! Glenda is also connected to good lenders and inspectors who can facilitate the ENTIRE real estate transfer process as smoothly as possible. Experience matters, and Glenda's got it. I will be working with her again."

~ Terry C.

"Glenda provided extremely useful advice along with a personable touch that made my family immediately comfortable. Glenda listens and adjusted our search criteria based on our needs and wants. With her assistance, we were

able to purchase a nice place at a good price that we will be happy with for many years to come. Thank you!"

~ Daniel S.

"Glenda was AMAZING! She was a pleasure to have as our real estate agent. When we saw our listing, we were blown away! Her hard work and knowledge of what it takes to sell a home paid off! A few hours after listing our home we received multiple offers! She walked us through every step of the process. She was patient and kind with us. We highly recommend Glenda Koernig for your real estate needs. You won't find a better agent! Thank you, Glenda!"

~ Juan & Gloria F.

CHAPTER 19

SHOOT FOR THE MOON

" WE HAVE BEEN DILIGENT IN BUILDING OUR OWN SYSTEMS AND CREATING DELIVERABLES TO OUR CLIENTS. WE DO THIS WITH THE BELIEF THAT OUR CLIENTS ARE NOT TRANSACTIONS, INSTEAD THEY ARE PEOPLE!"

KENE MBA
AUSTIN, TX

GET TO KNOW KENE MBA

My name is Kene Mba. I am the broker/owner of NuView Realty Group LLC, a residential real estate brokerage licensed in Texas. My family and I have called the great state of Texas home for over 17 years, the last 5 years of which have been in the eclectic and ever-dynamic city of Austin, TX. My wife and our 3 kids live at our home in Pflugerville, a diverse and fast-growing suburb of Austin.

I got interested in real estate as an investor over 13 years ago after my wife and I bought our first rental home in the Houston, TX area. At first it was a curiosity and a means to get into investing for our future, but it became a powerful tool for us, and the passion only grew from there. When I left my corporate career in 2015, I decided to go full time as a real estate salesperson and property manager with a zeal to help as many individuals and families as I could to get into the home of their dreams, or to sell their existing homes and move their equity to new homes, or to satisfy pressing personal needs. Having helped hundreds of people since, dozens of which I have personally represented, I can confidently say that home ownership or selling a home is often one of the most important decisions that people take.

Connecting with community area businesses is a great way for me to grow my networks and in turn my business. I love to meet with local business owners and change-makers, so it was easy for me to become a Local Leader with Parkbench. I expect that these connections will lead to a thriving ecosystem of ideas, learning and sharing of community leaders and organizers of positive change in my environment.

SHOOT FOR THE MOON

KENE MBA

"I felt heard." These are the words that make my real estate business different from most others. These are the words that have become the beacon for our business. These are the words I live for.

Our business model is based on one thing: "Everyone is an individual and should be treated as such." It's not fancy but it is powerful! At NuView Realty Group, we strive to have every client feel special and address them as individuals with issues and concerns that are unique to them.

People are attracted to our group because they know we are not a 'run of the mill' operation. It's not enough to just be heard as providing a full, customized client service is the end goal.

We have been diligent in building our own systems and creating deliverables to our clients. We do this with the belief that our clients are not transactions, instead they are people!

PEOPLE FELT RUSHED

Opening my new business during the Covid 19 Pandemic, I was fraught with challenges of many sorts. People felt rushed into making hasty decisions about their purchases. There were delays in shipping materials for renovations or new home builds. Uncertainty was at the core of our business world as the economy is now being pushed into high inflation which has created another flux in people's behaviors.

The sense of anxiety created a real estate market full of uncertainty and out-of-proportion housing prices. A mentality of "take what you can get" became a common catch phrase as people were forced into bidding wars with upwards of 20+ other offers as low inventory was prevalent.

Understanding that the real estate market is cyclical, I know that the market will settle in time. What I don't know is how long we have to wait it out. Now faced with inflation and high interest rates, we have to adapt to another set of 'rules.'

We really need to close our ears and eyes to what the media has to say about the market. It's their job to sell their services and they are at the forefront of creating the high anxiety that people are feeling. We need to change the dialogue and get back to helping our clients make good decisions based on solid facts.

EDUCATE WHERE I CAN

As a professional real estate agent, it is my duty to educate my clients but I still have to stay in my lane. This is to say, I can not give advice regarding mortgages or legal matters or anything outside the scope of my license and training. I do however, refer my clients to professionals that I am in contact with or have worked with on previous dealings.

The home buying process has a lot of moving parts so I believe it is my job to help them navigate this. I help them understand all the, sometimes confusing, parts like;

- The pre-approval process for a mortgage.
- Inspection vs appraisal of a home.
- The contract elements.
- The responsibilities of a home buyer in terms of providing documentation to lenders and lawyers.
- Conditions of sale.
- Owner's title policy.

- How to negotiate a contract.
- The need for an environmental survey, if necessary.

In the end, the question has to be asked; *"Do you really want this house? If so, let's play hardball!"*

INVESTORS- A DIFFERENT KIND OF BEAST

Before I got my real estate license, my wife and I owned a couple of rental homes in Houston, TX. We had mixed success with these rentals, especially as we had to evict our tenant in one of the houses and later went on to sell the house. Just before we let go of the house, I left my 9-5 job in Nigeria (oil and gas industry) and went to Colorado for a graduate degree in engineering.

This was during the US recession of 2008, and I decided to sell 90% of my liquid asset portfolio in preparation for what was coming. Good thing as the market crashed only a few weeks later. It was then I decided to move my investments into rental properties. As I gained knowledge of real estate investing, I learned my approach wasn't following the proper model, so I was advised to sell both units and we did just that.

Fast forward to 2015, I left my corporate job for good and went full-time into real estate. I bought three houses in the Houston area and became a silent investor in an apartment complex. In April of 2016, I bought into a franchise model of property management and then obtained my real estate license.

I learned patience when I was working with investors as they have different ways of thinking. They are tough to work with and some think they are more educated than they actually are. They can also be very demanding because it's all about numbers to them.

For example, the average home buyer looks at six homes before making a decision, whereas an investor can look at twenty plus homes which can take several months. Furthermore, investors tend to research online for information, which is disorganized to say the least. Now, I present myself as a real estate agent, not a real estate investor.

GO BIG AND GO FAST

I signed up with an investment group that is highly organized and proficient. It is a fee-based organization and is designed for the serious investor.

It's important to keep in mind to first understand what your goals are when investing in real estate. Do you want to supplement your income or are you interested in creating retirement income? Whichever space you want to play in, create a plan and stick to it.

If you want to create a retirement plan, then the rule of thumb is to go big and go fast! You don't want to play on the sidelines dabbling with one or two houses. You want to get to the point of buying whole apartment buildings. It's like a real-life game of monopoly!

HOT AUGUST NIGHTS

My wife and I love Austin. It's a vibrant city with a cool vibe. Unique to this area are the limestone cliff formations that are found throughout the city. The Colorado River flows through the heart of the city, creating a series of lakes that stretch for more than 100 miles. Austin's climate is subtropical and boasts an average of 300 days of sunshine each year. It can reach over 100 degrees during the summer months, but we enjoy more moderate temperatures in the winter.

The locals like to talk about their mountains (rolling hills), but to be honest they are more like 'pretend' mountains. I liken Austin as a 'small California city within the state of Texas. Its politics are liberal and the people are accepting of diversity and inclusion.

In the last three years we have noticed a large influx of California residents moving here. This could be in part due to big tech companies setting up here. Apple, Oracle–and even Elon Musk(Tesla) have made Austin their 'home.'

Austin has set itself up well to receive these high tech companies because the infrastructure is in place. With zero state income tax, people realize the financial advantages of being here. Also, the University of Texas is becoming a business think tank as venture capitalists make their way to assist with tech start-ups.

If you are thinking of making Austin your home, you can look forward to a decent standard of living where your dollar goes a lot farther than most large cities in America.

CONTROL OVER MY DESTINY

As mentioned, I initially got my real estate license to off-set the fees when buying and selling my own investments. I knew this was how I wanted to build my retirement. I was in search of a business on the side that would complement what I was already doing and I wanted to be passionate about it as I would be doing it for the better part of the next 25-30 years.

My grandparents always owned their own business, which laid the groundwork for my determination to be self-employed. Stemming from their inspiration, today I have a real estate broker license and I am enjoying working with honest, hard working people.

I want to pay my own bills at the end of the day and I want to have control over my own destiny. Thankfully, my real estate business checks off all the boxes!

9-DIGITS CLUB

I do have plans to grow and expand my business further as I am building a team of professionals between Houston and Austin. I currently have one agent in Houston working under my brokerage but I am wanting to run my local business in Austin for a few more years before taking on new agents.

I'm looking for between ten to twenty-four agents to join my team over the course of several years. I would rather hire slow than fire fast so I will be particular about who I bring onto my team. Initially, I will be recruiting newer agents or agents who have two to three years of experience. My wish is people will want to stay with me and build a long-term career vs switching around brokerages due solely on commissions.

I have never been attracted to the large, national brokerages, instead I prefer to build my own brand even if it takes a little longer. I am relying heavily on creating customized solutions for my clients so I want to groom my new agents to align with these values. The training will be directed towards creating a sustainable business model based on relationships and referrals.

Real estate, in my opinion, is not to be conquered as some may think. Instead, I want my agents to reflect on what *Ben* or *Susan* wants and ensure that they are heard and 'seen.'

Ultimately, my endeavor is to create a *"9-didgits club"* which will achieve 100s of millions in annual sales. Keeping in line with having an intimate group of people all with the same goals and passions, is my idea of a solid business.

GETTING MY NAME OUT THERE

Not by accident, I recently joined on with Parkbench as I saw the value that it can bring to my business. It will help me get out there and meet new people and help small businesses owners in my community. The videos and social media impact can only help make my brand top of mind and offer me and my agents a real opportunity to make an impact at a local level.

I look forward to going to more community events and contributing to my church more. As for social media as a business tool, it too keeps me top of mind and offers followers a chance to glimpse into my business.

SHOOT FOR THE MOON, LAND IN THE STARS

As an immigrant to America, I have been blessed with many opportunities and continue to be. Although I am a work in progress, I am a self-determined individual building my future. My motto is based on "If you shoot for the moon you may land in the stars." I have lofty goals, but nothing is going to stop me from pursuing them, even if I have temporary set-backs.

> *"How can you accomplish your 10-year plan in six months?"*
>
> ~ PETER THIEL

In my opinion, your goals should be set high- high enough to get you out of bed everyday!

I want to thank a few people who have been instrumental in supporting and encouraging me to stay on track and reach for the stars.

My mom was one of the most compassionate and empathetic people I have ever known. My dad is a strong-willed individual who taught me to never fear obstacles. He instilled confidence in me that I may not have otherwise had. Thank you both for everything! I miss you mom.

Chioma, my wife, and my three children, I thank you for your patience and understanding when I was traveling and working away from home. I am building my life around you now and don't want to miss another minute!

Kene Mba

REACH OUT TO KENE MBA

kmba@kenesellsatx.com
www.nuviewaustinrealty.com
Facebook: www.facebook.com/kenesellsatx
Instagram: www.instagram.com/kenesellsatx
LinkedIn: www.linkedin.com/in/nuviewrealtygroup/

WHAT CLIENTS ARE SAYING ABOUT KENE

"Above five stars goes to Mr. Kene. His great personality, passion, patience and ability to get questions answered made my home purchase experience rewarding. Definitely attentive to my style of homes, step by step guide and advice helped my home purchase dreams come true. Thank you, Kene! I recommend Kene for your home buying journey. "

~A'retta J.

"Excellent professionalism. I am honestly impressed by how proactive and accessible Kene was with his services. I trust my rental will be a long endeavor with Kene. Thank you."

~ Mazi. C.

"Kene was more than willing to take me from house to house looking for a house for my boyfriend. He is very helpful as he printed me out an itinerary

and map of all the places we were to go. He turned a displeasure into a pleasure. I recommend Kene if you're in need of a good Realtor®"

~Karen H.

CHAPTER 20

LET'S GROW LOCAL

" Demand for sustainable housing is growing worldwide. Material supply chains and energy costs based on finite resources have reached their limit. As the climate becomes more inhospitable, we need more efficient solutions. Climate refugees will necessitate the rapid building of new communities and the reinforcement of existing ones."

Jason Heidenescher
Columbus, OH

GET TO KNOW JASON HEIDENESCHER

Jason Heidenescher is an experienced real estate broker with a strong background in finance. Jason is an investment specialist, spending several years as a proprietary trader and owner of an investment research firm. Jason is a trusted resource with over 24 years in Finance and Real Estate.

Ohio REALTORS® President's Sales Club Award of Excellence

Columbus REALTORS® Ten Million Dollar Club

NAR Green Designee

New Construction Specialist

Custom Home Specialist

Investment Property Specialist

Jason will listen to your needs and help you find the perfect new home. With strong negotiation skills to maximize value and return on your investment, Jason can help guide you through the process to closing and beyond!

Columbus REALTORS® Member

Ohio Association of REALTORS® Member

National Association of REALTORS® Member

Multiple Listing Service of Columbus REALTORS®, Inc. Member

LET'S GROW LOCAL

JASON HEIDENESCHER

Born and raised in the Midwest, mostly in Central Ohio around the capital city of Columbus, I'm familiar with family values and hard work. Our area has a proud heritage as an industrial and manufacturing powerhouse. We have robust infrastructure with world-class logistics, and the capacity for future growth. Our strong talent pipeline is sustained by many renowned educational institutions in the area. More than 10 top engineering colleges are within a five-hour drive. Purdue University, the University of Michigan, Michigan State University, Carnegie Mellon University, the University of Kentucky, and of course the Ohio State University, to name a few.

With leading universities and top-ranked liberal arts colleges, the Columbus region boasts one of the highest concentrations of college students in the U.S., totaling more than 134,000 students. Of those moving to the area, 42% are college graduates. One of the youngest and most educated populations in the country, and the only one in the top 10 in the eastern half of the U.S. The Columbus metro ranks first among large Midwest metro areas for population and job growth since 2010 and is among the fastest growing metros in the country.

Keyvan Esfarjani, Intel's executive vice president, chief global operations officer, and general manager of Manufacturing, Supply Chain and Operations, explains, *"You can have the best kind of regulatory environment and the best land for use, but you need to have a pipeline of talent. Columbus, Ohio, is a great place for diverse talent. It's also around schools and has a population of folks who are very tied to the Midwest. They want to be there; they want to solve problems.*[1]*"*

We are a one-hour flight from 60% of Canadian and American populations. Within a day's drive (10 hours or less) from the Columbus Region, 46% of the country's population and 48% of headquarters operations can be reached. Located 10 miles south of Columbus is one of the world's only cargo-dedicated airports, Rickenbacker International Airport, which can help import and export goods any place, any time. FTZ 138 (Foreign Trade Zone) encompasses the entire Columbus Region and is legally considered outside of customs territory. That means goods may be brought into the site without formal customs entry.

With businesses looking to reshore and secure their supply chains in North America, Ohio becomes a natural choice. We're not only central for distribution, but we have a diverse economy ideal for companies like Intel to build out their supply chain. The Central Ohio metro area has absorbed some 130% of the state's population growth since 2000. Columbus itself is a national product test market, as our demographics closely match the average population. We get to try things first and if it flies here, it goes nationwide. Centrally located between Chicago and New York, Columbus boasts the greatest market access of any major metro.

Like many communities across the United States, Central Ohio has a shortage of affordable housing. Unlike other communities, Central Ohio is getting a major tech employer offering an average salary of $135,000 per year. As you would expect, home values are rising, and builders can't keep up with demand. As the population is expected to roughly double by 2050, to over two million, something has to give.

This is where the solution is found. A local, grass roots organization is bringing affordable, renewable, safe, carbon negative housing to Central Ohio, the Midwest, U.S., and all North America. Demand for sustainable housing is growing worldwide. Material supply chains and energy costs based on finite resources have reached their limit. As the climate becomes more inhospitable, we need more efficient solutions. Climate refugees will necessitate the rapid building of new communities and the reinforcement of existing ones.

As the world builds the equivalent of an entire New York City every month, reducing the carbon emissions of material is critical to combating climate change and controlling costs. While we've made great progress improving the energy efficiency of building operations, the next frontier is reducing embodied carbon in buildings — the emissions from material manufacturing and construction processes. Construction is responsible for over 40% of global emissions, rivaling transport and non-building manufacturing COMBINED.

Extraction and transportation of these materials is a large source of both emissions and cost. Creating local, circular supply chains accomplishes both goals simultaneously. By eliminating transportation, we can focus production on local consumption. This keeps profits in the local communities and increases economic growth. Nearly half of all cargo transport is fuel for energy. Think about that for a minute. A similar story exists with construction.

The current style of single-family home construction has existed since the 1800s. While great gains in efficiency have been found, the general style is much the same. The cost of these efficiency gains is the issue. We are sacrificing our health, our planet, and our local economies.

Current construction wall system designs for residential housing employ an airtight approach consisting of multiple layers. Lumber framing is installed first. Market supply is tight, volatile, and difficult to ramp up in times of need. *"The U.S. only makes about 60% of the lumber that it needs. Of all Canadian lumber, approximately 65% goes to the U.S. In Canada, 50% of all lumber is made in British Columbia. British Columbia has the problem with the pine beetle and the lack of future timber supply. There is not a lot of room for more supply to be manufactured, so along with the demand-side of home building is the supply-side constraint, and more expected supply constraint coming. It takes 80 years to grow a*

Lodgepole pine tree.[2]" Waste is high, carbon output for logging and shipping is high, supply takes a long time to grow, and much of this material is treated with toxic chemicals and imported. Canada loses its old growth forests, contributing to mudslides and loss of natural habitat. Fewer trees equals more CO_2 and faster climate catastrophe.

The next installation is OSB (oriented strand board), a toxic mix of wood chips and glues pressed together in a massive factory with a gargantuan press. Even tighter supply than lumber and more toxic, this product faces the same issues as lumber but worse. "*The price of OSB has increased 510% since January 2020, exceeding the peak price increase in lumber by nearly 180 percentage points. In addition to elevated prices, acute shortages have plagued the residential construction industry. OSB accounted for roughly two-thirds of wood panels used in wall sheathing in 2019.*[3]"

The third layer is the weather barrier, usually made of petroleum-based plastic. From Dupont, "*Tyvek® can be safely incinerated and, under optimal conditions, will lead to only the release of water and carbon dioxide, leaving no residue. In fact, it can even be used as fuel, yielding more than twice the energy value of coal, and as much energy as oil, in terms of BTU rating.*[4]" This highly flammable, "*100% synthetic*" material serves a very important role in current wall system design, as this must protect the wall system from water intrusion and potential for toxic molds. Improper installation of the weather barrier can invalidate the entire wall system design. If the weather barrier fails and water intrudes into the wall cavity, it can't escape and will find a ready source of food for mold.

One of these food sources is the fourth layer in this wall system design, the insulation. From Building Science "*To avoid mold problems, avoid water problems. Design and build in a manner that reduces water problems. Mold also requires food. The food it likes best is cellulose — the more processed the better. Mold really likes wet paper. It kind of likes wet wood, but not as much as it likes wet paper. It likes processed wood better than it likes real wood. So, mold likes oriented strand board (OSB) better than plywood and plywood better than a stud or a joist. We've always had some moldy buildings. But more recently we are building with different materials in different ways that lead to more mold and different mold. We use paper-faced gypsum board instead of plaster and lath. We use OSB instead of wood boards or plywood. We use much more insulation. The typical person also spends more time indoors now than 50 years ago.*[5]" Fiberglass insulation is also an irritant and "*the International Agency for Research on Cancer has classified some fibers used in fiberglass as possible human carcinogens (cancer causing agents).*[6]" Another type of insulation, "*Rigid-foam sheathing is made from extruded polystyrene, or XPS. This produces CFCs, which have been determined to damage the ozone.*[7]"

The fifth layer in this current wall system design, as noted, is drywall. Drywall is a ready food source for mold and a ready source for the landfill. Waste in drywall installation and renovation is a main toxic landfill contributor from construction. "*According to the EPA, once that construction is finished, most scraps are sent directly to landfills. There, gypsum becomes wet, mixes with other organic materials, and turns into hydrogen sulfide, a rotten, egg-smelling gas lethal to humans in high doses. The compound can contaminate water and raise its acidity—a risk to marine and freshwater animals.*[8]" This product is also high in carbon output, damaging to the environment when mined, dangerous to the miners, a tightly controlled supply with regular price fixing allegations, and after a weather event like flooding, it's a total loss.

"*As Hurricane Katrina raged through New Orleans in 2005, neighborhood after neighborhood collapsed from flooding. Of the houses that stood, many still had to be bulldozed due to mold within the walls. But one building, a plantation-home-turned-museum on Moss Street, built two centuries before the disaster, was left almost entirely unscathed. The Pitot house was built the old way, with plaster walls,*" says Steve Mouzon, an architect who helped rebuild the city after the hurricane. "*When the flood came, the museum moved the furniture upstairs. Afterwards, they simply hosed the walls—no harm done.*[9]"

The sixth layer in this wall system is siding. Another petroleum-based plastic, "*Vinyl siding is made from polyvinyl chloride (PVC), which is not biodegradable. Many environmental organizations have called for a ban on PVC because its production releases dioxin, a deadly toxin that can harm both humans and animals. Stone is a non-renewable resource and requires a lot of labor to haul and install.*[10]" Another common option, "*Hardie board is manufactured under extreme heat, which is not good for its carbon foot-*

print.[11]" Fiber cement boards also must be cut, releasing silica dust, which is dangerous to inhale. Brick is a third common option, *"It takes immense heat to manufacture brick. The clay bricks are baked in kilns for days at over 2000 degrees. Brick is very heavy. If you order brick from a remote locale, it will increase the environmental impact of the product because of the fuel needed for transport.*[12]"

Much of this material is also synthetic, created with dangerous chemicals that slowly off-gas into the indoor environment. Glues, resins, plastics, fireproofing materials, and others can cause serious and long-term health issues. That new car smell or new house smell can be dangerous. *"Formaldehyde is a chemical used in the production of adhesives, bonding agents, and solvents. For this reason, it is commonly found in a variety of consumer products including pressed-wood products (plywood, particle board, paneling) and foam insulation.*[13]"

The solution is a natural material building system distributed across the country for short, local supply chains that minimize carbon output. Offsetting imported foreign materials with locally sourced materials will create jobs and provide income for rural economies. This material is fire resistant, pest resistant, mold resistant, non-toxic, renewable, recyclable, and carbon negative. Supply can be sourced locally and increased rapidly as needed. Unlike a tree which takes decades to grow, hemp can be harvested in as little as 60 days.

Hemp gives farmers a valuable rotation crop for a new advanced biomaterial industry. This crop requires fewer inputs and has been shown to increase yields of crops that follow. Known for millennia as the strongest natural fiber and an excellent source of plant-based protein, hemp has another contribution to make by way of the hurd or shiv.

Hurd is the woody core of the hemp plant stalk left after the fiber has been removed. Having a high silica content, hurd can be mixed with lime and water to create hempcrete. Hempcrete is a natural insulation material with all the above properties. Hempcrete does not burn, it registers a zero for flame and smoke spread. Hempcrete contains no chemicals that can off-gas into the indoor environment. Hempcrete is made with lime which has a high pH (alkaline) and acts as a fungicide. Lime is naturally antimicrobial and repels undesirable insects like termites. Hempcrete is moisture permeable and absorbent, naturally regulating humidity efficiently. There is no wall cavity to trap moisture and no food source for mold. We don't fear water or try to repel it. We let the wall absorb and release moisture naturally.

Hempcrete also has thermal mass inertia that creates efficient temperature distribution. Much like a hot rock in the sun or a radiant-heated floor, hempcrete helps maintain a consistent temperature throughout the structure. These two properties, natural humidity regulation, and thermal mass inertia decrease the required HVAC inputs by half, further lowering the carbon footprint and operating costs of the structure in the future. The solid mass wall eliminates thermal bridging — the loss of effective insulation value created by stud framing which breaks up the insulation in a standard wall system. Solid precast interlocking blocks leave no gaps or holes in the building envelope. This mass also functions as an excellent sound-proofing material.

Building with hemp can capture 130 kg of carbon dioxide per cubic meter. One hectare of hemp crop will consume over ten metric tons of carbon dioxide annually while the plants grow, four times more than a hectare of mature trees in a forest. A 2000 square foot house constructed with hempcrete blocks will lock up over 10 metric tons of CO_2.

In the U.S., "*In order to fill an underbuilding gap of at least 5.5 million housing units during the next 10 years, while accounting for historical growth, building would need to accelerate to a pace that is well above the current trend, to more than two million housing units per year.*[14]" At ten metric tons of CO_2 per home, that's a potential 20 million metric tons or more of CO_2 that can be sequestered in the walls of homes per year. With local supply, we can do it at a fraction of current costs.

Hempcrete works for commercial buildings too. France just completed the Pierre Chevet sports centre. South Africa just built the tallest hempcrete building in the world, a seven story, multi-use with residential above commercial. Many other structures dot Europe, Australia, Canada, the U.S., and even Japan. The oldest standing hempcrete home is found in Japan, built in 1698. The oldest hempcrete structure in Europe is a bridge in France, constructed between the years 500 and 751.

Help spread the word! What is old will be new again. Every structure built is more CO_2 sequestered. Farmers are ready to grow this crop. Centralized extraction is only for centralized profits. Local supply chains make sense. Hemp is hyperlocal. Come grow with us. The solution grows like a weed. 🙂

Jason Heidenescher

REACH OUT TO JASON HEIDENESCHER

Jason Heidenescher
H Real Estate
Broker Owner
NewHomePartner@gmail.com
newhomepartner.com
biomaterials.us
(614) 701-6236
g.page / NewHomePartner
facebook.com / JasonHeidenescherYourNewHomePartner

WHAT CLIENTS ARE SAYING ABOUT JASON

"My wife and I have had the pleasure of working with Jason for more than 5 years now, following a chance inquiry regarding a home for sale. Since then, he has helped us find our starter home, and when the time came, he worked to find what is now our forever home. Always patient, kind, and genuine, he took extra care to listen to our needs, while helping steer us confidently through the home buying process. We couldn't be happier to have him as our trusted realtor and friend!"

~David H.

"Jason has facilitated the purchase of 2 luxury condominiums in Dublin, Ohio for me. He was thorough, informative, patient and a top-notch professional throughout all of the negotiations. He managed to procure fair market pricing

on both properties, while ensuring my interests in both quality and maintenance issues. He has gone the extra mile in helping me find tenants for my rental properties, and he has accumulated an excellent team of service professionals in everything from property photographic marketing to finish trim repairman and general handyman. His assistance has been invaluable, and I look forward to future ventures with him. He is the kind of man you maintain a relationship with after the transaction, because his knowledge, expertise, integrity and kind heart are characteristics difficult to find amongst his contemporaries. I highly recommend Jason for all of your real estate needs. You will be pleased with the interaction and results both."

~Michael D. C.

"I have been working with Jason for over 4 years and he was instrumental in getting us our home in Dublin. He was also instrumental in finding us investment properties in Columbus and Dayton. He is someone you can trust and is very professional in his relationship with other agents. I strongly recommend him if you are looking for an agent that is trustworthy, responsive, and knows the real estate market in this area."

~ Ray A.

---

1. *Why Intel chose Columbus, Ohio to build chips - TechCrunch*
2. *There will be new bottom lumber price and 15 years of very robust building*
3. *Price of OSB Up More Than 500% Since January 2020 | Eye On Housing*
4. *Tyvek® - Advancing Sustainability*
5. *RR-0211: Mold—Causes, Health Effects and Clean-up*
6. *Fiberglass Fact Sheet*
7. *8 Green Siding Options Compared: Most Eco-Friendly Siding?*
8. *An Exciting History of Drywall*
9. *An Exciting History of Drywall*
10. *Environmental Impact of Different Siding Options*
11. *8 Green Siding Options Compared: Most Eco-Friendly Siding?*
12. *8 Green Siding Options Compared: Most Eco-Friendly Siding?*
13. *Formaldehyde in Your Home - EH*
14. *Housing Is Critical Infrastructure*

CHAPTER 21

CASUALTY OF SUCCESS

" I treat each listing like a new business I just acquired. As the CEO of this new company, I need to invest in it and optimize it for our target market."

John Grafft
Chicago, IL

GET TO KNOW JOHN GRAFFT

Realtor® John Grafft successfully advocates for his clients by putting their interests ahead of his own and creating relationships. He's an award-winning marketer, trained negotiator, and teacher of teachers for first-time home buyers. He finds off-market deals for seasoned investors and protects his clients long after the contract is signed. He's been honored by the National Association of Realtors® as a "30 under 30" Realtor® and has been recognized as a Top Producing Broker by the Chicago Association of Realtors® since 2012. He is a contributor to the real estate section of *Forbes* and has been featured in *WSJ*, *Crain's*, *Curbed*, *U.S. News* and other publications.

CASUALTY OF SUCCESS

JOHN GRAFFT

Chicago's a city of neighborhoods. There are 77 in total and each one has its own character and authenticity that's felt everywhere from the housing to the restaurants. I reside in Old Town, but over the years have lived in Lincoln Park, Lakeview, and the Gold Coast. Chicago has culture, great public transit, and illustrious universities, but something that really touches my heart is the proximity to Lake Michigan. Most mornings, whether it's 0 or 100 outside, I get up, wipe the sleep from my eyes, and go for a walk to the lake with my wife. Our lakefront path goes from one end of the city to the other and you can see three states from the beach. The water brings a calming effect, but once you enter the underpass below Lake Shore drive, you open to a world of new energy, with runners beating their best time, pelotons keeping pace, and daring swimmers who choose the lake over the pool every time. And this goes on all day!

Walking back, you're bound to encounter a gaggle of children walking to school, young professionals rushing to the train, and scooters zipping by going to and fro. The bell hasn't rung at the stock exchange, yet the accomplishments already had, are bountiful and inspiring.

I became a real estate broker after a series of bad experiences with

Realtors®. After getting locked out of an agent's car, being upsold, pushed into neighborhoods I wasn't interested in, and ultimately being offered magic mushrooms when they couldn't sell me an apartment, I wondered what world I just entered. This all happened in under 72 hours! Through these escapades I learned the structure of the business, and while I was only 19 years old, I was intrigued. Two years later I hunkered down, studied, and passed my real estate license. It was 2009. I was 21.

I couldn't find any established agents who would mentor me. I interviewed at apartment-finding agencies and they didn't want to hire a student. I wondered if I had made the wrong decision. I took the test, but finding an opportunity was more difficult than I imagined. Before discouragement really mounted, I started calling the numbers on For Rent signs to see if the landlords would pay me a commission if I found them a tenant. I drove through the streets everyday seeking For Rent signs. I would compile a list and then go home and call them. I made around 50 calls and reached 11 people who would listen to me. Five agreed to work with me if I brought them a tenant. It wasn't much, but it was the start of something.

That was 14 years ago. From there I gained a number of clients who would work with me for years to come. The rental side of the business was a good starting point, but I wanted something more challenging. I wanted my actions to have a deeper impact. A few of the professional landlords I met were buying lots to build homes on. We were in the midst of a financial collapse and land was cheaper than it had been in the two decades prior. At the time, I didn't understand why they gave me a shot. Maybe it was the constant stream of renters I was bringing to their buildings, or maybe they wanted to give a young person an opportunity, but after I asked, I received. I got a new construction home to sell. It was magical.

I started learning the process. I asked the developers to give me as much exposure as possible. I sat in on meetings with architects, contractors, and designers. I was on site watching the foundation form and was there when the insulation was blown in. I expanded my lexicon and learned the builders' lingo or at least, I tried my best to. I remember on one of my first showings I said the countertop had a waterfall edge. It didn't. A more experienced agent was kind enough to tell me the difference in private instead of correcting me in front of their clients. I learned a lesson in professionalism that day. The agent could have easily called me out and earned some credibility with her clients, but instead, took the high road and saved me the embarrassment.

It's been a long time since that first showing. I remember my hands clamming up, flutters in my stomach, and dry mouth like I just ran a marathon. Today, I have emotions every time I show a home, but they're of a different variety. I treat each listing like a new business I just acquired. As the CEO of this new company, I need to invest in it and optimize it for our target market. Simultaneously, I spend hours walking through the property deciding what to say, how to say it, and where to say it. I decide the tour direction, so we move from one point of interest to another, doing my best to avoid lulls in attention. I learn everything possible about the property. They aren't just wood floors, they're 3 ¼" rift cut, white oak with a naked stain. The walls aren't white, they're paper white with an eggshell finish to make clean ups easier. The countertops aren't quartz, they're Calcutta Prado Quartz from MSI, imported directly from Brazil. Yes, the cabinets are soft close and have under cabinet integrated illumination but check this out — the inside of the carcass is lit too so you can see exactly what you're looking for! This attention to detail and masterful presentation is what a luxury buyer is looking for when they tour a multi-million dollar home. They aren't looking for "*And here's the kitchen. Check out the backyard. I'll be returning emails if you need anything.*" They want to be enthralled and charmed; captivated and entertained. You want to see the "High Heart Rate" notification light up on their iWatch as you tour the property. This attention, care, and ability to promote is the reason one client after another refers me to their friends and family.

Being a relationship and referral-based agent was something I decided I wanted early in my career. Any agent can hand their credit card information over to Zillow and start working with buyers, but that didn't interest me. Growing a team but treating it like a business where the goal is to make the most profit off each product (team member), didn't seem good for the team members or my clients.

I wanted to create something that stood out for good reason: a higher echelon of service and accountability that would rival the most esteemed lawyers, accountants, and consultants. That's easy to say but learning how to do it took me a decade. You can look left and look right in this industry, gleaning what your competition is doing and imitate it, but that felt disingenuous. To me, research and development felt more like rip-off and duplicate.

I'm good at selling, demonstrating, and marketing. That's what my clients hire me for. They have the choice of thousands of Realtors® and they chose me. That's a special feeling. I wanted to give every person I sold a home — with and every buyer I found a home — with the same special feeling I felt when they hired me. If they could feel like they got the best Realtor® and in kind, the best service, communication, and results, then they would refer me with trust to the people in their circle because we all want the best for the people closest to us. Win, win.

In 2020, I put a full-time videographer on the payroll to make videos for our listings. The plan was for me to walk through each property and explain what made the home special. For some it was the neighborhood, for others it was the building materials, but every home has something unique that stands out. We all know what happened next. As I watched the world change, I saw my favorite places close and some, ultimately shutter. It was devastating. I don't have a car and therefore spend a lot of time in businesses in between meetings and showings. I'd have a coffee here, a tostado there, but the commercial spaces of Chicago were my homes when I wasn't selling homes. My favorite businesses closed, and I felt impotent, unable to do anything to help. At 11:11 pm on a Friday the idea came to me. Promote the places I love by doing interviews with the owners and tell their stories. Let the public see the person behind the brand and understand what they sacrificed to make their dream happen. I had the equipment and the team. The next step was putting it altogether. This is when I started the My Chicago series. At the time, it didn't even have a name. Since then, I've been meeting with local entrepreneurs and telling their stories. I never thought I would learn so much from this experience. Sitting down with people who have accomplished so much, while at the same time meeting with people just starting their journey, has been eye opening for me.

Those conversations empower and fuel me to harness my inner grit and grind. The same mentality I had when I started is still imperative to have every morning when I wake up. Everyone was a naysayer when I told them what I wanted to do. I was encouraged to take the safe route. Embrace the W-2 and enjoy your 401k. There's nothing wrong with that, but it never appealed to me. Maybe I wasn't office bound, but more so I saw an opportunity for betterment. Comfortable, tenured agents grimace at the expense and effort of getting a floor plan made for their listing, thinking the property will sell itself. Many agents from the "Put it in the MLS, put it in the Paper, and Pray" generation don't see the need or understand the value of having 3D tours and video walk throughs. They don't appreciate showmanship and take for granted the miracle it is that they're in the position they are. I see the casualties of success in my field as the agent's reputation from yesteryear fuels the success of tomorrow; but today the resolution that carried them here is waning as contentment has settled in and hubris has rooted. That cycle can last a long time, but eventually the dwindling of effort, quality, and resources for their clients will come full circle and make room for agents willing to do more for buyers and sellers.

I hope you enjoyed reading this and hopefully it will help you put wind behind your sails in the tumultuous but rewarding career path of real estate.

John Grafft

REACH OUT TO JOHN GRAFFT

Contact info: (855) 4 - GRAFFT
Website: www.ChicagoRealEstate.io
Social media links: https://www.instagram.com/grafftrealestate

WHAT CLIENTS ARE SAYING ABOUT JOHN

"John Grafft is a special breed of Realtor®. You can tell instantly that he loves what he does, and his passion is reflected in his expertise and professionalism. He is well-connected, honest, and incredibly knowledgeable. I trust everything he says — do yourself a favor and put him at the top of your list the next time you're looking to sell or buy."

~ Isabel C.

"John worked with my wife and me to help us find and close on our first house in Roscoe Village. To say that he goes above and beyond is an understatement. In a historically competitive Seller's market, he helped us lock in the home we wanted, at a price within our budget, and in one of the most competitive neighborhoods in the city. Even the Seller's broker readily admitted we couldn't have closed without John's persistence and tact. Beyond just negotiating the best deal for us, John has proven to be an invaluable source of knowledge and advice for us in all things homeownership related as we navigate our first home. With his background in construction, he has a technical familiarity with building materials, repair processes, home systems, etc. that sets him far above other brokers and allowed us to genuinely feel at ease during each home

tour, inspection process and final walk through. We closed on our home last week and while for most client-broker relationships closing is typically the end of the road, John has been in contact with us daily helping us get settled in our new home and making sure we're set up for success as new homeowners (we pepper him multiple times a day with questions and he responds within seconds). His network of contacts is representative of his status as a top tier broker in the City — every attorney, contractor, engineer, etc. he's introduced us to has been a 10/10 both in terms of work product and pricing. While our plan is that this is our forever home, we joke that we would sell the house just to work with John again. He is absolutely the best of the best - if you need a broker for your first or tenth home (buying or selling) who is incomparably knowledgeable, responsive around the clock, well-connected and easy to spend entire afternoons with house hunting, look no further."

~Sam J.

"John is a true professional who was invested from day 1 in helping us find our first-time home. He was very responsive and knowledgeable about Chicago market. We hit the ground running and was under contract in less than a month, and John guided us through the entire process, from finding a lender, to negotiating a deal, to closing."

~ Kevin L.

"We just bought our first home and could not be more grateful that John was there to help us through. Not only is he incredibly knowledgeable about the market, but he uses a consultative approach that helps you truly understand what you're looking for and what's important to you. The best part about John, though, is that he's a fierce advocate for his clients; we ran into some issues during the buying process and John was there every step of the way working his magic in the background. Being able to trust your realtor is priceless. 10/10 would recommend."

~Jacque K.

CHAPTER 22
STARTING OVER FROM SCRATCH

"I LIKE REAL ESTATE BECAUSE I ENJOY FINDING HOUSES FOR PEOPLE AND THE DETAILED WORK INTERESTS ME. IN PARTICULAR, I APPRECIATE THE PROFESSIONALS I WORK WITH WHO ARE VITAL TO MY BUSINESS."

ROB YALE
GANANOQUE, ON

GET TO KNOW ROB YALE

Rob Yale is a people person who is excited by the idea of connecting people with their dream home. In fact, Rob developed an interest in Real Estate while buying his own home. Born and raised in Toronto, Rob understands the different neighbourhoods, and their particular nuances. Rob prides himself in his ability to focus on difficult problems to their eventual completion. Additionally, he has a great deal of technical know-how assembled through years of IT experience.

In his previous career, Rob worked as a professional composer and keyboardist specializing in music for games. His work in the music business included years of performance and recording with such diverse acts as David Bowie, Bruce Cockburn, and Jane Siberry. As well as working on music albums, he has performed on numerous film and television projects. Throughout the late 80s and 90s Rob built and ran his own recording studio, developing a reputation for being on the leading edge of technological developments in the field of audio. His experience as General Manager of his studio honed his organizational skills. Music requires groups of people to work harmoniously. Rob brings his well-rounded background in music to the field of Real Estate.

STARTING OVER FROM SCRATCH

ROB YALE

Although I have over six years of experience in the real estate industry, my path has led me down some interesting roads. I began this journey by obtaining an honors degree in English Literature from the University of Toronto-Woodsworth College. During this time, I was also heavily involved in digital music production which offered me countless opportunities to work with some of the best entertainers, including David Bowie.

I also have a passion for creating things that are useful, such as 3-D objects like vases and plant pots. I tinker with 3-D printers, and I am looking forward to finishing my latest project of building one myself. Photography has always been a favourite hobby of mine and recently I have taken to using drones to further my skill and knowledge of the art. If this isn't enough, I have my pilot's license too, however, I am now flying my drones most of the time.

FROM SCRATCH-AGAIN

During the COVID-19 pandemic my business faltered so I decided to take a hiatus from real estate until things settled down. My wife and I discussed the idea of pulling up our roots and we started perusing the town of Gananoque.

Moving from my community where I was established to a much smaller town where I don't know a soul was a leap of faith, but I am ready for the challenge. I feel confident in building my sphere of influence because I have great tools which include the Parkbench website and platform. Integrated with YouTube, the Parkbench system is perfect for me as I enjoy producing video content. In addition, I get to meet new people and build relationships that will then lead to a large database of people; something every real estate business needs.

I also want to expand my YouTube channel with content that local people in my town will find useful. I want to post stories about how to meet people and start from scratch, so others can benefit from my experience.

A FAMILY AFFAIR

My business 'partner', Carol Teichman and I have worked closely together for several years. We are distantly related through a close family tie, so we trust each other implicitly. Although we define our relationship as a working relationship, it may become a more formal partnership in the future.

I like real estate because I enjoy finding houses for people and the detailed work interests me. In particular, I appreciate the professionals I work with who are vital to my business. My sister and brother-in-law are both real estate lawyers who have handled many of my clients' dealings. I think because I have so many family members involved with the business it makes it a true family affair.

I interact well with mortgage brokers, bankers, house inspectors, and many other professionals. Every agent needs to have good working relationships with their 'team' because it really takes a village to complete every transaction. Now that I have moved into a new area, I am working on enlisting new professionals into my business. I am using recommendations from people in the area and sourcing Google reviews. Then I prefer to meet with them for a coffee and if it works out, I give them a referral. But the work is not over yet as I 'test' the waters and wait for feedback. Two things that matter most to me is the quality of the work they perform and their reliability because I need to know I can count on them to do a great job for my clients.

BUILDING MY FOUNDATION

As I am in the process of starting over, I am getting all my ducks in a row. I know I have to get out there and meet new people, so I am working with the Parkbench platform to speed up this process while building a new sphere of influence. Interviewing our local business owners and other people of influence will help me gain a foothold in the community.

I also make good use of an app called Nextdoor. I can post my video content there while making online connections with my neighbors. It directly connects people who are in your local neighborhood — as close as your next door neighbour! I will be asking people on the app, "Who wants to be interviewed?" and I am sure I will get a positive response.

Video is the cornerstone of doing business today. Outside of real estate, many businesses are using it and gaining clients. Inside real estate, video allows the 'walls to come down' as it were, even before you physically meet potential clients. With video, people feel like they have already met you before the handshake occurs. Leveraging video will give me a needed advantage in the marketplace.

GANANOQUE

In Gananoque it is easy to start conversations but hard to end them. Everyone is so friendly and outgoing and all it takes is a walk with my dog, Heather to experience this. It is a small town of just over 5500 people, and it is the gateway to the 1000 Islands. It is internationally known for eastern Ontario's most stunning waterfront communities and is visited by thousands of tourists every year.

The name Gananoque has several meanings including, "Water Rising Over Rocks" and "Garden of the Great Spirit." It is also at the intersection of the St. Lawrence and Gananoque rivers which are important waterways for the supply line in this area of Canada.

'Make a Life, Make a Living' is a local initiative by the township to enhance the current business storefronts and to support new businesses to the area. Its primary goal is to populate the vacant properties with thriving businesses and promote entrepreneurship.

For people looking to live here, you can expect a life of quiet peacefulness and connection. The area is rich in history and cultural experiences and the township offers countless events for all to enjoy. A local favorite is the free concerts in the park and with my musical background, who knows, maybe I will play there someday!

Early in the year, my wife Pat and I were looking at the houses for sale here and we both found the same one — independently from each other! So, we hopped into the car and bought it that same weekend. That's how quickly someone can fall in love with this little gem of a town!

SUPPORTING MY COMMUNITY

I've been thinking about the idea of joining our local Rotary Club in Gananoque. It will be a great way to meet a lot of new people and contributing to the community. I am looking forward to being involved with the farmers markets and the various charity events held here each year.

One of my neighbours is a town councillor so he is on my list of people I want to interview. I also have access to the mayor of our town so am looking forward to rubbing shoulders with these influential people as well.

STARTING CONVERSATIONS

When you love what you do, you want to do it more. Looking back on my career, knowing what I know now, I definitely would have started in real estate a lot sooner. Why? I love working in this business and I wish I had more years doing it.

One thing I have learned that has served me well is simply to say,

"Hello." All too often this simple gesture is all that is needed to start conversations that can ultimately lead to new business, new contacts, or even a new friend. Regardless, make it a habit and become a conversation starter and if it helps, get a dog — always a great way to engage passersby.

My approach with my business is more of an organic nature. I really don't enjoy door knocking or cold calling as these tend to be less personal and less effective.

TO SUM IT ALL UP

As I enter my sixth year in the real estate industry, I can't help but think about the people who have supported and encouraged me along the way. My wife and friends and most importantly, my clients, both past and present. I thank you all for being with me on my journey.

Rob Yale

REACH OUT TO ROB YALE

Sotheby's International Realty Canada, Brokerage.
85 Charles Street South
Gananoque, ON K7G 1V9
Canada
647-209-6464
rob@robyalerealestate.com
http://www.robyalerealestate.com/

REFLECTION

HOW TO BECOME A LOCAL LEADER® & GET MORE REFERRALS

" The riches are in the niches"

Grant Findlay-Shirras
CEO, Parkbench

GET TO KNOW GRANT FINDLAY-SHIRRAS

Grant Findlay-Shirras is the CEO and co-founder of Parkbench Inc. headquartered in Toronto, ON, CDA. Originally from Vancouver, when Grant moved to Toronto, he found himself without a network and sphere of influence — the most important thing for an entrepreneur. As a result, he, and his wife (Amanda Newman), created a neighbourhood-centric website to start building relationships with local small business owners. The idea worked and they became a household name in their neighbourhood very quickly . . . and this got the attention of Amanda's competitors — fellow real estate agents. Agents asked Grant and Amanda for their technology and blueprint and that's how Parkbench was born!

Parkbench became a multi-million-dollar tech company within three years and since 2014 has now served over 7000 agents in four countries. His mission is to help one real estate agent in every neighbourhood, worldwide, build their business through relationships, referrals, and community engagement.

Before Parkbench was started, Grant was a consultant and entrepreneur in multiple industries: fitness, nutrition, events, and travel. Over the span of the next few years, Grant was awarded several accolades including recognition as a top Thought Leader to Follow by Thrive Global, and Epic Impact recognized Grant as a 30 under 30 influencer. After starting Parkbench he was accepted into the 500 startups accelerator program in Silicon Valley, as well as the National Association of REALTORS® Growth Accelerator, REACH Canada: an accelerator program that helps launch innovative technology companies into the real estate marketplace. He was honoured to receive the valedictorian in his graduating class of 2021.

Grant is very passionate about community and business success, so Parkbench is the perfect marriage of the two. His drive for helping his clients create successful and sustainable real estate businesses is paramount. A strong community can only be created by the people who live and work in the area. That is why this book is both timely and important for the industry today.

The authors within this book have shared their most relevant strategies and commitments to their craft and Grant is proud to have spearheaded this project.

HOW TO BECOME A LOCAL LEADER® & GET MORE REFERRALS

GRANT FINDLAY-SHIRRAS

As we draw to a close, take a second to reflect on the stories, anecdotes, tips, and advice given to you by local real estate experts!

What are you going to START doing?
What are you going to STOP doing?
What are you going to DO MORE of?
What are you going to DO LESS of?

I ask my team these questions ALL the time, and every time we do this, we always figure out what tweaks to make to move our business forward, faster.

And I promise if you take time to reflect and ask yourself these questions, right now, and every month, you will figure out how to grow your business and live a better quality of life.

Now, as I take a moment to reflect upon the amazing people who helped put this book together, from the agent/authors to the book designers and the writing team, I am filled with pride and hope for the future.

Everyday these real estate agents pour their heart and souls into their clients, ensuring they have the best experience possible, and as you can tell from these stories, they all have their own unique way of doing it . . . and so can you!

However, they ALL have one thing in common — they are not "just a real estate agent", they are a Local Leader® . . . and you can be one too!

WINNING BELIEFS

Leadership is not given; it is earned, and these agents have earned the right to be in this elite category. Real estate is a game of perseverance and determination. No one gets to be an overnight sensation in any industry, let alone real estate, however, by focusing on the right things, they have become winners.

If you focus on these five things, you will grow your business faster

- I need more **Contacts.**
- I need to start more **Conversations.**
- I need an Item of Value to **Give** People.
- I need to Build **Relationships.**
- I need a **Weekly Newsletter.**

You don't need to buy more leads. You don't need to buy more advertising. You don't need a new salesy script to convert someone. You don't need a fancy and complex business.

Keep it simple.

THE SIMPLE FORMULA

With those five beliefs firmly in hand, all you need is a simple formula to create a solid foundation and a sustainable business model to generate client recommendations and referrals, forever!

Start Conversations with People
+ Give value to them
+ Follow Up and Add More Value
+ Ask Questions to see if they need your real estate knowledge and services
= New clients via relationships and referrals

YOU CAN DO IT THE HARD WAY, OR YOU CAN DO IT THE EASY WAY

NOwhere in this book do you read about buying traffic or leads.
NOwhere in this book do you read about door knocking or cold calling.
NOwhere in this book do you read about any kind of PUSH Advertising.
NOwhere!

What you do learn about is how to build relationships.
What you do learn about is how to build community.
What you do learn about is a relationship and community building platform called Parkbench.com.

Now it's true that one can go about this business doing all the things that these agents are doing without the use of a powerful platform, virtual assistant support, and professional coaching and training.

The expensive way to build your business is through advertising.
The hard way to build your business is by doing it all yourself.
The easy way to build your business is by hiring a team and using software to do everything except relationship building, prospecting, and serving your clients.

It's your choice which path you take.

DIFFERENTIATION IN THE MARKETPLACE

How many times have you heard people say, "Real estate agents are ALL the same?"

It's unfortunate that most agents are painted with the same brush by homeowners. You and I both know it's not true. You're not all the same. And after reading this book, you can see more examples of how agents are different.

Now here's what you need to do if you want to dominate your marketplace

- DO different things
- ACT in different ways
- HAVE something different to offer

If you want to stand out and differentiate yourself from your competitors, you need to BE DIFFERENT!

And if it feels scary . . . you're on the right path . . . so keep going!

THE *'RICHES ARE IN THE NICHES'*

Another important aspect to note is these successful businesspeople also pick a geographic niche to focus on; specifically, certain neighbourhoods or small towns. You'll notice they do not try to serve a greater city area, because they all know the "riches are in the niches."

After working with tens of thousands of agents for over a decade, we've found the optimal size of a geographic niche, for one agent, is between 25,000 and 50,000 people. This could be a couple of neighborhoods in a big city, or a couple of zip codes, or a small town. The reason this works is because:

1. It's big enough where there's enough turnover in this area for an agent to make the money they want to make and live a great quality of life.
2. It's small enough where you can actually achieve the personal branding goal of "everyone knowing your name."

We have found agents have more success when their geographic niche includes the neighbourhood where they live because it's easier to make homeowners believe you're the local market expert if you live there, and that's the #1 reason why they select one agent over another.

If you need help picking the right geographic niche and figuring out an action plan for how to reach your income goals in that geographic area, email area@parkbench.com, and someone on my team will help you do this.

There's one thing I am certain of, and that is the riches are in the niches!

Grant

BECOMING A LOCAL LEADER®

NEXT STEPS

At Parkbench, we created a system for Becoming a Local Leader® that works and here are the fundamentals of our system.

Step 1 - Pick a geographic area you want to work in.

Step 2 - Create a lead list of "influential homeowners" in your area. These people can become your clients and refer you tons of business. For example: other professionals in the real estate industry, home service professionals, personal care professionals, small business owners, leaders of non-profits, and community groups.

Scan the QR Code below for a free list of the Top 30 people you should meet because they refer lots of business to real estate professionals!

Step 3 - Contact them and give them something of value that has nothing to do with real estate. Focus on building a relationship with them.

Step 4 - Follow up and add more value to them.

Step 5 - After you have given value, and built a relationship, contact them again and simply ask them if they have questions about the market, how to improve the value of their home, buying/selling/investing in real estate, and where they are at in their real estate journey.

Our Local Leaders® make, on average, three times more than the average agent.
This means a local leader makes more than $150,000 whereas most agents only make $50,000.

This simple process works for anyone, anywhere, and it can for you too!

NEED HELP?

The Parkbench Team has helped thousands of agents Become a Local Leader® and add 12 or more transactions to their business in the first year of working with us.

- We can help you choose the best area for your business.
- We can give you a lead list for the most influential people in your area to connect with.
- We can give you items of value to give the homeowners and business owners in your area.
- We can create local content for you.
- We can give you scripts and templates.
- We can give you training, coaching, and accountability.
- We can help you do video marketing, social media marketing, email marketing, and more.
- We have a team and platform that can save you time and money, and get you results faster.

Now here is something important to know (that we think you'll like as well)

- We only work with one agent per neighbourhood.
- We have a money-back guarantee.
- And we have hundreds of five-star reviews.

So, if you're interested in learning how we can help you grow your business, scan the QR Code below, fill in the form, book a time to talk with our local marketing experts, and let's get to work!

Made in the USA
Monee, IL
25 October 2022